NORTHERN

HUNGARY

NORTHERN HUNGARY

A Historical Study of
The Czechoslovak Republic

by

Sándor A. Kostya M.A.

Translated by

Zoltán Leskowsky

Published by
Associated Hungarian Teachers
Toronto, 1992

Copyright 1992
by
Sándor A. Kostya M.A.
Toronto, Ontario

No part of this book may be reproduced in any way, or by any means, without permission from the publisher.

ISBN 1-882785-00-2

Printed in the U.S.A.

Contents

PREFACE

PART I.

Backdrop to the question of Northern-Hungary

PART II.

Northern Hungary

PART III.

Fate of the Minority

ADDENDUM

Preface

The Origin of the Slovak People

If we review the historic events of the Carpathian Basin from the time of the Hungarian settlement to the present, we observe that for most of those centuries people in this region lived in complete social and economic harmony with the Hungarians. On closer scrutiny we find that for a period of eight centuries there is no mention of the Slovak people in any historical accounts. Not even an exploration of legends and chronicles reveals any hint of their existence.

Before the Hungarian settlement of the region, the northern areas of the Carpathian basin played host to a succession of Celtic, Kvad, Avar, Frank, and Moravian-Slav peoples. The Kvads, at the end of the second century, were destroyed by the armies of Marcus Aurelius (121-180) Roman Emperor who invaded the territory as far as present day Trencsén [1]. In the fifth century the Huns replaced the Romans. After the collapse of the Hun Empire, Avars arrived at the western slopes of the Carpathian mountains in several waves. The Avars in the eight century were conquered by the Franks. Then, in the ninth century, the Moravian Slavs established themselves as an 'Empire'. It was at this time that the Slavs entered the pages of history.

It was Prince Mojmir (830?-846), who expelled the Nyitra area Moravian ruler, Pribina, and set himself up as Mojmir I. While Mojmir was forging his new Moravian Empire, Pribina received refuge from the Francs and was appointed 'Comes' (Fortress Commander). But by the time the Hungarians appeared in the Carpathian Basin, the Moravian Empire was quickly disintegrating. The Czechs had disassociated themselves from the Moravians and succumbed to the Franks. The Moravians were then displaced by the Magyar tribes. Now squeezed beyond the boundaries of the Carpathians, the Moravians made one more attempt to regain some territory. They broke into Hungary, but in the Battle of Bánhida (907) the Hungarian forces destroyed their armies and shattered their empire. The 'Great

Moravian Empire', which had existed merely sixty-years, was extinguished.

Nestor (965-1116), a Kiev Monk, in his chronicle referred to the inhabitants of the Moravian Empire as 'Slavs'. Cosmas (1039-1125) a Czech writer does not even mention Slovaks in his work dealing with Slav nations. Similarly, the XV century 'Pozsonyi Jegyzék' refers to the inhabitants of the surrounding border areas as Slavs only. There is no mention of Slovaks. However, it often refers to the people of the region as Tót, Vend, Hungari-Slavoni, Slaven, Wenden, etc... The word "Slovak"[2], in reference to the present-day Slovaks, was first coined by Antal Bernolák[3].

The Slovak ethnic identity appears to have emerged out of groups of people already settled in the northern regions of the Carpathian basin and from those slavic peoples who migrated there for centuries after the Hungarian conquest. Following the Battle of Bánhida, the Árpáds, the X Century ruling house of Hungary, settled tribes of 'Kuns', 'Besenyös', and 'Székelys' along the frontier regions as border guards, and built stone fortresses to secure their territory. The relics of some of the fortresses can still be seen today.

In the XII century, Hungarian kings settled considerable numbers of Germans in the counties of Nyitra, Turóc, Trencsén, Liptó, and Szepesség. These were augmented by Bavarians, Saxons, Flamands, and Schwabs who cleared forests, mined, and later became active in industry and commerce. In the XIII century Polish, Czech, and Minor-Russian settlers arrived, followed by the infiltration in the XVI century of Vlach shepherds of South-slavic origin to the grassy slopes of the Carpathian mountains .

The first large-scale ethnic melange took place in the days of the Turkish invasion in the XV century. At this time thousands of Hungarians took refuge in the Northern regions. The history of the Northern regions reflects the lives of these peoples for a period of ten hundred years. The fate of the Hungarian, Slavic, and others who had settled there was shaped within the same framework, but the initial process of becoming a nation in the case of the Slovaks did not take place until the XVII century. It began during the era of language struggles, as the Slovak language was not uniform. During this linguistic turmoil, it was mainly the intelligentsia who assumed the leading role of the ever-strengthening Slovak cultural and national movement.

Samuel Czambel [4], the greatest Slovak linguist, considered the Slovak language not Northern but of South-Slavic origin. By the end of the XIII century a significant number of Hungarians and Germans became Slavs as a result of intermarriages. Their numbers swelled to over 200,000.

Upper-Hungary witnessed the development of three distinct Slovak linguistic and spiritual regions in its territory. The purest of these were the 'Middle-Slovak', whose area extended from the Vág river to the Csórba watershed. The educated evangelical elements of this group became the most faithful proponents of the Czech cultural and linguistic influence. In contrast, the people who were not affected by this cultural and linguistic influence, later became instrumental in creating a Slovak national autonomy.

The Slovaks, whose territory extended from the chains of the White Carpathians to the line of the Vág river, were adversely influenced by the Czech. As a result of the Czech assimilation techniques, this area became a breeding ground for the strongest anti-Czech movements. The unbreakable spirit of the Slovak priests, educated at the University of Nagyszombat, pitted them against not only the Czech, but the evangelical Slovaks as well.

The 'Eastern-Slovak', in the linguistic sense, strongly differed from the literal Slovak language. These slovaks call themselves "Slovjaks". The Eastern-Slovaks whose area extended from the Csórba watershed to the less defined boundaries of the Ruthenian ethnographic region. These Eastern-Slovaks, who inhabited the regions around the towns of Kassa (Košice) and Eperjes (Prešov) and settled in the counties of Abaúj and Sáros (Šariš), always share strong cultural, social and friendship ties with their Hungarian neighbours [5].

The modern slovak cultures, in search of their cultural and national heredity, pursued a three pronged historical theory. These theories, developed from Slavic, Czech and Slovak perspectives, often contradicted each other.

According to the general Slav theory, the infiltration of Slovaks in the southernly direction had preceded the separation of the other Slavic tribes. Accordingly, it proposes that the slovaks did not settle at their first stop, in the vicinity of Dévény, Modor, Nyitra, but proceeded southward inundated the southern part of Moravia as well as the Ens and Lajta rivers areas in the south. There is no historical or archeological evidence of such a large scale invasion having taken place.

The Czechs theory denies that the Slovaks, together with the Czechs, crossed over the Visztula and Ode rivers, the threshold of their ancient Slavic land, in racial, linguistic and social unity. According to Czech theory, the Slovak split from the Czech linguistic mainstream occurred while both groups were still in their Central European homeland and this transition took many centuries. The Czech linguistic claim is that the Slovak language is but a dialect of the Czech. Their theory presupposes that the Slovaks are Slavic-Czechs or perhaps Slavic-Hungarians! Their theory also states that the separation of the Slovaks from the Czech mainstream was caused by the appearance of the Hungarians along the valley of the Danube. The author of the modern Czech theory, Frantisek Palacky, regards this as the singular event which prevented the unification of the Northern and Southern Slavs and the establishment of a great Central European Slavic Empire.

The Slovak people accept only part of the Slav theory. According to their version the Slovaks separated early from the other Slavic groups in their ancient land and arrived to the area of the Mátra and Tátra mountains in the early part of the first century as a separate tribe. Historical accounts place the Czechs and Slavs in the Bohemian, Moravian and Serbian area no earlier than the VII century.

The Slovaks consider themselves the inheritors of the Great Moravian Empire. For example, the Slovak author Skulteti pictured the Danube as the southern border of the Slovak lands, extending from lower Austria through Dévény, Komárom and Esztergom. This border then extended further through the foothills of Mátra and Bükk all the way to Miskolc, then turned east along the Tisza and Bodrog rivers enclosing the Slovak areas towards the Polish border. From such geographic license, it is only a small step to the Safarik or Stur theory, or the most recently stumbled-upon "Pannonia theory", which elevate the Slovak tribe as the successor of the ancient establishment of all the Slavs.

"Slovak was the Lord along both shores of the Danube where it enters Austrian land", wrote a slovak poet, "all the way to the Black Sea, and from the Tátra mountains to Szaloniki!" However, this view is not corroborated by the emperor and great historian, Constantine, or any chronicler of the era. The Hungarian concept, substantially differs from these three theories by stating that the "Slovak" ethnicity developed only after the Magyar settlement of the Carpathian region and as a result of the amalgamation of various homogeneous peoples. Later, other cultural elements settled on this core, notably the Czech, Polish, minor-Russian and the Vlach. [6]

FOOTNOTES:

(Preface)

1.   The relics of the Roman era are on display in the Museum of Komárom.

2.   **Slovak** - according to the Historical Lexicon of Hungarian Ethnography, the ethnic designator "Slovak" was first used in 1828. Although the country of Slovakia was used as early as 1575, and appeared to be used in reference to the state of Slovania. Only after the First World War did the word 'Slovak' receive wide usage. Previously, the cultural colloquialism 'Tót' was used.

3.   **Bernolák Antal** (1762-1813) a cleric, author and language reformer. His most noted work, published in Pozsony in 1790, was the "Gramatica Slavica" (Slovak Grammer).

4.   **Czambel Samu** (1856-1909) a Slovak linguist, whose more important publications were "Tót Hangtan" (Budapest 1880), "Priskevky k denijám jazyka slovenského" (1887), "Slovensky Pravopis" (1890), "Rukovat spisovnej reci slovenskej" (Túrószentmárton 1902), "Slováci a ich rec" (Budapest 1903). His greatest and unfinished work, "A Tót nyelv és helye a szláv nyelvek családjában" (The Tót language and its place in the slavik language family) was published in one chapter and very limited edition at Turócszentmárton in 1909.

5.   "Magyar tájékoztató zsebkönyv" (The Hungarian Information Handbook) published Budapest, Societas Carpatho-Danubiana 1941, pg 173-174.

6.   Ibid, pg 172-176.

PART I.

BACKDROP TO THE QUESTION OF NORTHERN-HUNGARY

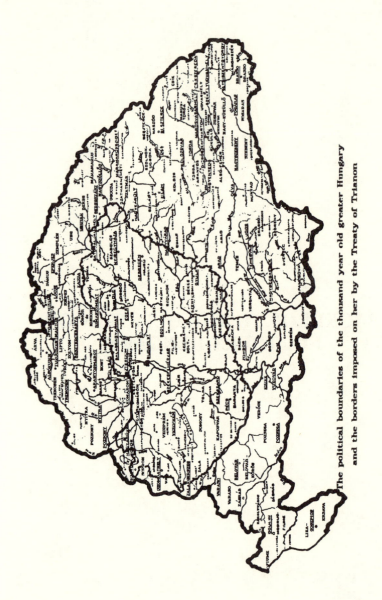

The political boundaries of the thousand year old greater Hungary and the borders imposed on her by the Treaty of Trianon

CHAPTER 1

The History of Slovak Nationalism

The XVIII Century leaders of the Slav peoples living in the Carpathian basin, fuelled by nationalistic ideas, along with Slovak and Serb intellectuals sought contacts with Czech intellectuals living beyond the Carpathians. As a result of the Czech influence, Slavic minorities came to regarded Czarist Russia as the chief patron of all Slavs. Their hopes were greatly fortified by the Balkan policies of Russian, and in her war with Turkey. This conflict, in which Russia meant to create the appearance of a "war of liberation" for the Slav peoples living in this area, was supported by Slavs living in the Balkans and the Carpathian regions.

The Habsburg Monarchy soon realised that the real aim of Russian politics was not to liberate the Slavic minorities in the Balkans, but to gain access to the sea. This they could only achieve by inciting unrest in Balkans among the Slavs by promising them national independence.

Katherine the Great (1769-1796), in the Treaties of 'Kuchuk-Kainarji' (1774) and Jassy (792) secured for her Russia the northern shores of the Black Sea. The Turkish Sultan was also forced to relinquished the Crimea to her and opened the Dardanelles to the Russian commercial fleet.

The Slavs living in the Carpathian Basin did not consider, that in the empire of the Czar, 'their paternal protector', numerous non-slav ethnic people lived under oppression. For example, the several million strong Ukrainians, who are descendants of the Avars and the Huns. Equally, it did not occur to the Slovaks of Northern-Hungary in that period, that the despotic Czarist regime was far from being democratic. They punished theirs own 'muzhiks' (peasants) with 'knouts' (whips), and sent the unsatisfied leaders of the oppressed minorities to Siberian for exile. The Czar's befriending politics succeeded in placing a vale over the eyes of the Slavs living outside of Russia.

The majority of the Czech leaders living in the Austro-Hungarian Monarchy were loyal to the Habsburg Empire. Neither the Czechs nor the Slovaks of Upper Hungary contemplated forming an independent state. Initially, these minorities only advanced linguistic and cultural demands to the Monarchy. But during the ensuing eighteenth century political upheavals, they began to envision independence for themselves from the Hungarian economy in some form of a tariff-free autonomy, but still under the authority of the Austrian rulers.

The Slavs were divided in choosing their loyalties; those leaning toward Vienna were called 'Austro-Slavs', while those attracted by Czarist Russia were referred to as 'Pan-Slavs'. The efforts of the Austro-Slav faction, after the Austro-Hungarian Compromise of 1867, were bent on forcing a similar political compromise between the Austrians and the Czechs. However, the strong resistance of Vienna frustrated their every effort. After lengthy power gamesmanship and factional politicking, Thomas G. Masaryk, a Czech intellectual, and Edward Benes, a Czech freelance writer, invented the 'Czecho-Slovak' State theory. With this fiction, they were able to unite the Pan and Austro Slavs shortly after the fall of the Czarist Russian Empire in 1917. Their aim was to unify the Northern and Southern Slavs into one empire, even if the expense meant the destruction of Hungary.

The embitterment of the nationality question in the Carpathian Basin was caused by the Pan-Slav political movement. As consequence to nineteen century imperialism and post World War I political instability, it became obvious that the European minority problem required solution to two leading questions:

1.   How can the problem of minorities within a national element be resolved in a mutually beneficial manner? ... and

2.   How can the affairs of cultural minorities spanning several established European nations be resolved?

The Irish, Basque, Catalan, and even the French Canadian (Quebec) independence movements are current and ongoing problems. In the present century, political resolve replaced theoretical and doctrinal examination of the minority problems. In effect, the minorities governed by their own notions of nationhood are lessening the chances for a lasting solution to their own problems.

The definition of nationhood bespeaks a stable, historically developed community of people sharing a distinct cultural, linguistic, economic and geographic commonality. Equally, ethnicity or cultural minority describes the association of a self conscious group of people, outside the majority, who speak the same language and share like customs. It is understood that cultural minorities like nations have the need and the right to organize along racial basis in such a way as to segregate themselves politically and in the judicio-economic sense from the state-forming nation. The intent of this book is not to redefine concepts or resolve in greater depth the conceptual and intellectual questions of history, but simply to explore and inform the public about two matters;

(a)   the development of the ethno-political history of the 200 year-old ethnic minority 'problem' in Hungary; and

(b)   the history of the unlawful dismembering of a thousand-year-old legitimate nation, its peoples and its territory into a historically illegitimate foreign state. Equally, the subsequent history of genocide inflicted upon the Hungarian peoples severed from their homeland and finding themselves as ethnic minorities in the embrace of foreign nations.

The linguistic-cultural movement is the central issue to the Hungarian minority question. In order to understand the minority problem one must first examine the political climate preceding the Slav linguistic-cultural movement. The first recorded minority linguistic demands surfaced during the 1790-91 Hungarian Parliamentary assembly, as a result of the earlier held Serbian Church Congress.

Part I

Among the participants of the May 1790 Serbian Church Congress in Temesvár (Timisoara) were found political and military representatives of Serb minorities. The clergy no longer dominated their own assembly. The senior officers lead by Colonel Secujac demanded the establishment of a separate Serbian country. Tököly Száva [7], a culturist-politician and a leader of the Serb minority in Hungary, in opposition to the military demands, advocated a peaceful compromise with the Hungarian majority in the spirit of constitutionality. However, the burning issue raised at the congress was neither linguistic nor cultural but whether to revamp their theoretical minority nation concept from a religious to a political one. The debate was long and heated, and in the end, the political and military coalition succeeded in redefining the nation concept from an orthodox to a secular one. In a petition to the Hungarian parliament, the Serb minority demanded the right to exercise linguistic and political autonomy. The very same year, the Romanian minorities also presented their linguistic and political wishes to the Transylvanian assembly known as the 'Supplex Libellus Vlachorum'.

While minority problems existed before, they generally manifested themselves in the form of linguistic and cultural demands. Interestingly enough, the minorities were not the only ones with linguistic concerns, the Hungarians also had linguistic demands of their own. They were tired of having German and Latin as their political, clerical and educational official languages. The Hungarian György Bessenyei (1747-1811), as early as 1777, urged for a purely Hungarian academy in Budapest .

Joseph II, Habsburg Emperor and Hungary's "King-in-hat", in the interest of forging a unified empire, and without regard for the political history of the member countries, or the diversity of the cultural minorities involved, issued a language decree on May 11, 1784. He ignored the Hungarian Constitution, and refused to have himself crowned as King of Hungary. He dismissed the constitutional parliamentary system, which existed in Hungary since the twelfth century. His draconian measures caused a backlash in the empire.

The language of administration in Hungary was Latin as late as the eighteenth century. While the Hungarian national assembly demanded that the Emperor make Hungarian the official language of Hungary, the Croatian-Slavonian minority presented a "Declaratio" (declaration) to the 1790-91 assembly, which vouched to uphold Latin as the empire's language of administration. The Croatian-Slavonian nobility protesting at the Vienna court in 1681, was dissatisfied by the fact that the Serbs living in the Monarchy received privileges, which the Croatian would never see fulfilled. One hundred and ten years later they protested against the introduction of the Hungarian language as a state language. They defended Latin, arguing that, the language of administration in Hungary should be Latin, and that it was unconstitutional for the Hungarian nobility and the Vienna representatives to force a Hungarian state language on the country. The "Declaratio" served to ignite the nationhood concept of a 'Great-Croatia' .

The demands laid down in "Declaratio" became the starting point of a conscious Croatian national policy. Parliamentary representative, Baron Ferenc Bedekovics (1755-1827), protested against introducing the Hungarian language as a compulsory subject in the schools of minorities and companion countries. He argued that the Croatian nation is as much true-born as the Hungarian, and it would be a shame if in time it had lost its language, and ceased to be a separate nation. And yet while Hungary struggled against the Austrian forced Germanization of her people, the minorities within her borders fought to support the Habsburg oppressors instead of the oppressed.

CHAPTER 2

The Slovak Nationality Question

In Northern Hungary, during the year 1790, the Slovak national question marked its birth. In that year, the Slav author and linguist, Antal Bernolák, in his work "Grammatica Slavica", argued that the Nyitra-Nagyszombat version of the Western Slovak dialect be accepted as the basis for the literal Slovak language. Two years later, in 1792, he founded the 'Literal Guild' under the name of "Towarisstvo Literarneho Umenia" to propagate his view. Juraj Fándly (1754-1810), the first Slovak culturist-politician, closed ranks with the language movement of Bernolák and joined the group of language cultivators in the town of Nyitra. While Bernolák and Fándly advocated a national idea akin to the French enlightenment, János Kollár (1795-1852) Slovak poet, and the Croatian Ljudevit Gáj (1809-1872) believed in the renaissance of Slav politics 'a la Herder and Hegel'.

During the course of the Nineteenth Century, the spreading 'Great-Slav' Theory inspired by German ideological sources manipulated the nationalistic movement in the Carpathian Basin. Just preceding this Great-Slav movement, there existed a Slavic cultural initiative based on a more consolatory French influence. This cultural budding could not develop due to the thwarting effect of overheated political passions of the period. A mystical 'Slav nation' concept, imported under German influence, dominated the minority movement. Borrowing its anti-Hungarian rhetoric from German political literature, the Slovak minorities and the Hungarian majority was drifting apart.

The leading advocates of change used pamphlets and clubs to advertise their views. The period's most notable pamphlet on the minority debate titled "Sollen wir magyaren werden?" (Must we become Hungarians?), was published in Gaj's Zagreb press. This pamphlet caused an unusual storm of controversy at the Prague Diet. Another voice, Kollár, in his first political pamphlet, titled "Uber die Magyarisierung der Slaven" (Notes on the Hungarianization of the Slavs) was passionately anti-Hungarian. Gaj, who was familiar with

Kollár's pamphlet and shared his political view and passion, willingly offered the services of his Zagreb printing facilities for the publication of similar works. Jiri Palkovic (1769-1850), a Slovak politician and cultural affairs critique, in 1812 at Prague, founded a literary club with the title, "Spolek Literatury Slovenske" (Slovak Literary Club). In him the Czechs found the first influential Slovak friend, when as a function of the club, Palkovic published a literary and scientific weekly, which propagated a series of articles advocating friendship with the Czechs.

While Hungary was governed by the Austrian Prince, Metternich, with Vienna's blessing the Slavs took advantage of the prevailing anti-Hungarian sentiment and intensified their "Great-Slav" propaganda. The Germans were quite willing to support this antagonistic atmosphere for their own political gains. It even became fashionable, as propagated in the teachings of Herder, to disavow the Hungarians both culturally and linguistically. In the 1820's, a journal titled "Geschichte unserer Zeit" (Today's History), published in Leipzig, became very popular. The journal editor, Henrik Schokk was raised in Northern Hungary and educated in the universities of Germany, which greatly influenced his political perspective. Upon receiving his diploma, he did not return to Hungary, but became a German journalist. In this capacity, he delivered a series of relentless attacks against Hungary for her "alleged" anti-Slav efforts and atrocities. The city of Leipzig by this time became a centre for anti-Hungarian Pan-Slavic propaganda. Sándor Rudnay's[8], "Slaves Sum" (I am a Slav), published in 1830, mobilized the lower strata of the Slovak culture behind the Pan-Slavic movement providing the movement with a major boost.

During the period of the language war, more than one hundred political pamphlets had appeared in Hungary dealing with the plight of the minorities. This extensive pamphlet literature had begun in Zagreb in 1814, with Chaplovich's "Der Sprachkampf in Ungarn" (The Language War in Hungary), and ended in Prague in the fall of 1848, with Michael Milosláv Hodzsa's pamphlet "Der Slovak", which urged the practical realization of the dreams of the 'Great Slavs'. Judging from their tones these pamphlets were aimed at confrontation rather than reconciliation. Seventy-five percent of the German language pamphlets of Pan-Slavic origin were published in Leipzig, even though Prague and Zagreb were the focal points of Pan-Slavism.

The reason for German publication of pro Pan-Slav pamphlets cannot be explained, because Hungarian censor laws at the time were very liberal. In the spirit and argument of these German language publications, one can recognize the influences of the universities of Halle, Jena, and Gottingen. The anti-Hungarian sentiments of Herder, Hegel and Schlotzer not only captured the interest of the Slovak populace, but it even beguiled such Slav intellectuals as Safarik.

From the 1790-91 Diet and the "Supplex Libellus Vlachorum", half a century had passed before the first concrete memorandum was submitted to Vienna, on behalf of the minorities. The petition was handed to Prince Metternich by Paul Jozeffy, the Lutheran priest of Tiszolc and head of an eminent Slovak minority leadership delegation. It requested the establishment of a Slovak Seat at the university of Budapest, the employment of Slovak censors, and urged for the re-institution of Latin as the language of religious administration in registering births, marriages and deaths. Because the submission of the Jozeffy Memorandum circumvented the Pressburg Diet, Joseph Palatine of Hungary through diplomatic means stalled the issue. The Slovakian nationality question would have taken a much more favourable turn in 1848, had the request of the memorandum "Wishes of the Slovaks" been granted. But the nobility, which went to the other extreme from its Latinistic cult, ignored it as much as it ignored Count Széchényi's precautionary academic speech delivered in the fall of 1842.

Against the backdrop of the 1848 Hungarian revolt, which was aimed at the Habsburg dictatorship, the Slovaks made their move. In the spring of 1848 at the instigation of Prague and St. Petersburg, the Slovaks once again declared their nationality program. Decidedly aggressive in character, this program was presented on May 10, 1848 at the Liptószentmiklós (Liptousky Mikuläs) popular assembly called together by Stur, Hodzsa, and Hurban, the Slovak political trio of 1848. The list of their demands and the program details were as follows:

1.   Use of all minority mother tongues at the Diet.

2.   Separate Diets to be held, and the ethnographic borders to be re-determined.

3.   The representatives are obliged to truly represent their voters' interest (in Parliament).

4.   Slovak be the language of judicial trials and public meetings in the Slovak ethnic districts (Okolie).

5.   Slovak schools and universities to be established.

6.   The Slovak language to be taught in other ethnic districts , as well as,

7.   The use of a Slovak flag to be allowed, and Slovak to be the language of command for the Slovak National Guard.

8.   Freedom of press, freedom of speech, right of assembly.

9.   Statute labour to be abolished, and the agrarian problem settled.

The first two points of their program had already been met by the revolutionary 12-point declaration of Pest, in the March, 1848. The rest of the demands could have been settled through direct negotiations. However, the creation of a separate ethnic district, with a separate National Guard, a separate language of command could not have been reconciled within the prevailing Hungarian constitutional view. The Pan-Slavic Congress of Prague in June 1848, and the West-Slovakian uprising organized by Hurban with Viennese support during the September-November period of the same year substantially hindered the chances of reconciliation. Matters became worse when the Hungarian government employed troops, aided by a substantial number of Slovak volunteers, to suppress the uprising. These events provided the historical reason as to why there were no worthwhile negotiations between the leaders of the Hungarian liberation movement and that of the Slovak nationalist movement in 1848.

During the first weeks of Austrian victory in the 1848 revolt, the Viennese government was willing to offer some personal rewards. Patronage was provided to the University of Vienna to finance the publication of Slavic newspaper, such as the "Slovenski Noviny" (Slovakian News), which under Kollár's editorship tried to please the Imperial Censure, and the "Vistnik Rusinov Austrivskoj Derzavy" (Paper for the Ruthenians of the Austrian Empire), which opportunistically served the Austrian interest. However, after the death of Kollár in 1852, the Pan-Slavic movement failed produce another pro-monarchist leader to succeed him. The Slovak separatists of Northern Hungary, turned away from Vienna in disappointment. The strongly biased pro-Czech school policy of the Minister of Education, Leo Thun, the only prestigious Austro-Slav, was too much for them.

After the 1848 revolt, the Royal Patent of Kremiers (Kromerz, a Moravian town) and the Olmutz Manifesto, simultaneously issued on March 4, 1849, effectively nullified the Hungarian constitution. The Patent declared that the territorial unity of the Habsburg Empire and its subject countries were indivisible. Following the imposition of the Olmutz Manifesto the Austro-Slav leaders, who supported Vienna, found themselves in a difficult situation. Stur retired with a nervous breakdown, while Hurban and Hodzsa were placed under the political restraints of the 1849 Manifesto. Minority leaders, like Saguna, Janku (Romanian), Gaj (Croatian)and Jellasics (Croatian), disappointedly turned away from public life. The people of the various nationalities and minorities in the Carpathian Basin were subjected to the greatest Habsburg oppression.

In September 1850, the "Dienstes Instruktion", a Bach's public administrative edict, was issued from Vienna. The directive divided historical Hungary into five parts: Kronland Ungarn, Vojvodina, Translyvania with Partium, Croat-Slavonia, and the Frontier Areas. Hungary proper was then further subdivided into five districts: Pest, Pozsony, Sopron, Kassa, and Nagyvárad.

The Bach Hussars practiced extreme cruelty, and the and their tyranny knew no limits. One by one all the minorities, including the Hungarians, fell silent under the Austrian yoke, and showed no substantial political initiative until the Austro-Hungarian Compromise of 1867. After the Compromise, the aims of the Pan-Slavic movement manifested themselves in parliamentary debates, attempting to focus exclusively on minority problems.

CHAPTER 3

Pan-Slavism and the Hungarians

After the defeat of the 1848 Hungarian War of Independence against Austria, the forces of Viennese despotism turned a deaf ear to the nationality question. For more than a decade the Emperor ignored the unresolved problems of the minorities. The October 20, 1860 'Royal Diploma' served the consolidation of despotism by proclaiming promises instead of concrete directives. The proclamation made some rather illusionary concessions. It restored the integrity of Hungary, and recognized its pre-1848 institutions, but at the same time, it established an Imperial Parliament for joint administration of common affairs. The February 1861 'Royal Patent' limited the number of delegates that could be sent to the Imperial Parliament. Hungary and Transylvania were allowed 85 and 26 representatives, respectively. The Hungarians and Transylvanians unanimously rejected the very concept of the patent. Their representatives noticeably stayed away from the Reichsrat, the common parliament. In light of the obvious nature of the Royal Patent, the Hungarian distrust for the Viennese Court became complete, especially, when it was apparent that the Patent gave the Czech Parliament full political rights and powers while abolishing those of the Hungarian Parliament.

Preceding the years to the Austro-Hungarian Compromise, one discovers that the necessity of such a compromise between Austria and Hungary began at Solfeirno. The various nationalities within the empire had to be restrained by separate armies. The young emperor, Franz Joseph, could not afford to antagonize the rebellious Hungarians while trying to restore the former great power status of his empire, maintain his rule in Italy, and fight for the leadership among the German-speaking countries. He also had to appease the Pan-Slavic movement, which flared up with renewed vigour in Hungary shortly after the Compromise.

In Lombardy, which was defended by Colonel Joseph Radetzky of the Imperial Army, the volcanic forces of Italian

28

nationalism were at work unabated. Here, as in Hungary, Austria had to maintain a rule of tyranny. Threatened by revolts from within as well as from without, Austria maintain ruthless civil and political order in the empire. Through the political genius of the Italian statesman, Camillo Cavour, the Kingdom of Sardinia relentlessly embarrassed Vienna. The Crimean War had alienated Russia from Franz Joseph, and Prussia became a secret enemy. Then, as Sardinia managed to secure the support of Napoleon III, Austria's political isolation became complete. By 1859, the Emperor of France himself directed the joint Franco-Italian forces against the Austrian army, and defeated it soundly at the Battle of Solferino on June 24. Franz Joseph was forced to give up Lombardy. By the November 10, 1859 Zurich Peace Treaty, Lombardy together with Tuscany and central Italy became part of the Italian Kingdom under the House of Savoy ruled by Victor Emmanuel.

In the aftermath of Solferino the weakness and instability of absolutism became obvious. The Austrian army due to rampant corruption among its suppliers were not fed or armed properly. It became evident that the imperialistic aspirations of Austria had pushed the empire into a military and financial fiasco. The Austrian Army and the Bach administration proved to be the most expensive of its kind on the Continent. Hungary was swamped by Austrian centralists and masses of Czech federalists. The Czech political leaders had a Pan-Slavic orientation, the ordinary Czech seemed to "forget" about their national dream and tried to become good Austrian citizens. Bach's staunchest helpers and supporters were the Czechs.

The October constitution of 1860 did not meet Hungarian expectations. Even though in the "permanent and irrevocable low" the emperor did give up absolutism and centralism (at least on paper, and in principle), and revived the old constitution based feudal diets, he still superimposed upon them the imperial council and the central parliament (the Reichsrat), which dealt with mutual matters.

The Royal Diploma and Patent elicited a mixed reaction among the nationalities and minorities. Among the Hungarians they stiffened the spirit of resistance, and started an era of active opposition. While the minorities saw their own advantage in the preservation of the status quo. Through Russian and Czech instigation, the minorities question in

Hungary received a new inertia. The strengthening ties of mutual trust, which developed in the 1850's between the Hungarians and the Slovaks quickly eroded. And while the Pan-Slavic movement during the period of reconciliation had been underrated by the Hungarian politicians, the leaders of the minorities had taken it very seriously.

The Slovak Nationality Program of Turócszentmárton (Martin) exceeded the Serbian resolutions of Karleva (Karloca) in the extent of its demands. It demanded not only territorial autonomy and equal national rights, but also the acceptance of their own language as the exclusive official administrative and educational language in its particular ethnographic locality. The Karleva (Karloca) Congress did not claim such an extensive language right, probably because of the multilingual character of the Vojvodina.

The Pan-Slavic efforts and demands gradually became major opinion-forming factors among Czech, Slovak and Serb minorities in Hungary. Only the Hungarian upper class, or "the establishment" ignored the nationality question. While governmental agencies paid only a perfunctory attention to the new Minority Bill and tried to delay its enactment, a far-reaching event took place in Russia. Moscow and St. Petersburg became the site in May of 1867, for the Pan-Slavic Congress. It was attended by some three-hundred Czech, Serb, Croat and Slovak grass-root delegates from widely varying economic, political and social backgrounds. The Czarist Government acted merely as 'host' and 'advisor' to the participants.

This Pan-Slavic Congress unintentionally prepared the way for the outbreak of World War I. The radicalism of the budding Slovak-nation concept began to unfold during this congress. For example, owing to the effect of this Pan-Slavic Congress and that of the Serb-Illyr movement, Stephen Moyzes, Bishop of Besztercebánya, a participant and principle patron of the Slovak nationality movement in Hungary, admitted mainly Slovak theologians to his county seminary, and demanded a knowledge of the Slovak language from his Hungarian pupils.

During this stormy period, Hungary was seized upon by Austrian centralist and German political influences, in order to justify the so-called 'Dualism' or administrative harmonization of the two states. The real consequence of the 1867 Compromise[9] was that Hungary strayed from the road of social progress by abandoning the populist spirit of 1848. The country lacked the necessary democratization, without which a reconciliation amongst the peoples of the Carpathian Basin could not be achieved. In retrospect, the Parliamentary Act, Act XII, of 1867 turned out to be a tragic obstacle in the constitutional, social and minority discord of Hungary prior to the First World War.

CHAPTER 4

After the Compromise

The Austrian Compromise of 1867 escalated the minority unrest in Hungary. Slovak leaders became more vocal and focused in their political demands. The cultural maturing of ethnic minorities gave a stronger voice to the Pan-Slav ideas of Bernolák and Stur. Initially, the Matica[10] at Turószentmárton, only prepared and published Slovak readers and textbooks for Slovak courses authorized in the grade and high schools of Nagyröce, Turócszentmárton and Znióváralja. Later, it began to publish selected poems of Holly[11] and Sladkovics[12] for the Slovak intellectual class. There was a hope that the feeling of resistive passivity would lift and in regions of large ethnic minority population, the Hungarian and Slovak intellectuals would move closer in a mood of mutual respect and understanding.

In the initial years of the twentieth century, the old passivity gradually changed into a nationalistic movement. During the elections of 1905, held under the government of István Tisza, the Slovak National Party suffered a major setback. Milan Hodzsa representing the electoral district of Kulpin, was the only Slovak elected to the Parliament. The next year however, the Slovak Party's parliamentary representation received a seven fold boost. Immediately, the newly elected party members immediately joined their Rumanian and Serbian counterparts in the Club of Minorities and professed solidarity with all Slavs and the Pan-Slav movement. Almost overnight the Slovak National Party changed its name to "Slovenská Národná Ludová Strana". A cleric, Hlinka[13], who was also a strong supporter and budding leader of the Slovak minority movement, received parliamentary recognition and support from a Slovak Member of the Legislation, Srobar[14], who represented the electoral district of Rozsahegy (Ruzomberok). Because of his anti-Hungarian views, Hlinka quarrelled constantly with his ecclesiastic superiors. The Bishop of Szepes suspended his priestly functions and summoned him to an audience. On his return from Szepes, Hlinka delivered a strong subversive and anti-Hungarian address at the Rozsahegy railway station, for which he was immediately arrested. Srobar linked to Hlinka's instigation was also detained. On November 20, 1906, Hlinka and Srobar were convicted on charges of subversion and instigation to riot. Both men were sentenced to one year in prison. Because of mounting public displeasure with the judicial proceedings, Hlinka was released on probation. Dysfunctional cooperation between Slovak minorities were evident during this period. For example, in December of the same year, disagreements arose between the minority Slovak politicians of Budapest and those of Turócszentmárton. Hodzsa[15] and his people expected a solution to the mounting minority tension from the Viennese supported Slovak leadership, residing in Prague. While Milan Hodzsa was striving to enhance the nationalistic consciousness of the Slovak minority, increasing number of Czechs and Slovaks began to heed more and more attentively the idea of a 'Ternary Federation' proposed by Ferenc Ferdinand, Emperor of Austria, heir apparent to the crown of Hungary. Meanwhile, the Hungarians, Gábor Ugron [16] and Lajos Láng [17] were also working on a confederation concept, which was to form the basis for an Austrian-Hungarian-Czech Monarchy.

Parliamentary disturbances increased as the minorities gained parliamentary seats. During the January session of the 1907 parliament, the debate for the extension of the Austro-Hungarian Suffrage Reform Bill was disrupted by the politically active young Czechs, who launched motion to legalize parliamentary voting by secret ballot. Outside the parliament, to give greater voice to their cause, a pro-Czech publication was started under the name "Nase Slovensko" (Our Slovakia) for the propagation of "Ceskoslovenská Jednota" (Czechoslovak unity). Jehlicska, a Slovak Member of Parliament, to provide more parliamentary distraction, resigns his seat over alleged foreign harassment of minorities.

The anti-Hungarian drive by the minorities continued relentlessly. In 1907 on July 13, a Pan-Slav Congress was convened in Prague. The Hungarian government did not attach great importance to it, even though the intensified activity of the Slovaks proved quite evident. For example, Hlinka, a priest and a Hungarian citizen, set out on a lecture tour of Bohemia and Moravia. His theme was the political status of the Slovaks minority in Northern Hungary. The tour was approved and sponsored by Stojan, the Archbishop of Prague, and Blaha Marian, Bishop of Bruna (Brno). Both men strongly supported the concept of closer cooperation between the Czechs and Slovaks. During his tour, Hlinka made several lecture stops, one in particular at Czernova. Anticipating a large turnout, the Pan-Slav propagandists day in advance of his arrival began to agitate the local minorities. On October 27, 1907, the excited mobs, waiting for Hlinka, threatened the authorities present. The police responded with the use of firearms. Nine people died in the confrontation. Even though the lengthy investigations clearly showed that the basic cause for the incident was the unrestrained agitation of the Czech propagandists, the immediate effect was a deterioration beyond repair between the Hungarian and Slovak ethnic relations. Hlinka once again was arrested and jailed for public disturbance.

The Pan-Slavists, in order to solicit foreign support, published his November 30th farewell letter to Hodzsa in the American Slovak papers. International sympathy was further received from notables, like Björnson Björnstjerne and Tolstoy. Bjornstjerne, a Norwegian journalist, in December of 1907, wrote an article for the Munich periodical "März", in which he sharply criticized the minority policy of the Hungarian government and refused to participate in the European Peace Conference. Leo Nikolajevich Tolstoy also protested strongly against the Czernova bloodshed. On the home front, Milan Hodzsa, while in the Hungarian chamber of deputies, raised strong protests against the Czernova incident. Count Andrássy, Minister of Interior Affairs, repudiated the charges, and blame the agitators and the threatening mob for creating an atmosphere of confrontation.

Another Pan-Slav Congress was held in Prague, in late August of 1908, this time in the spirit of "Neo-Slavism". A new breed of Pan-Slav politicians appear on the scene. At the congress, 80 Slovak, 35 Serbian-Croatian and 160 Polish representatives were present. People like Dr. Karel Kramar, a university professor and Czech representative of the Vienna Reichsrat, wrote supportively of the congress. In his pamphlet "The Slav Conference in Prague", Kramar described the basic principles of Neo-Slavism. In this same year, the essay of Edward

Benes, "Le Probleme Autrichen et la Question Tcheque" saw publication in Paris. It described the political struggle of the Slav minorities in Austria. In his study, Benes proposed the federalization of Austria and recommended full autonomy for the minorities. The relentless Slovak propaganda produced pamphlets and books in German, French, English, even in Esperanto. A pamphlet discussing the lot of Slovaks in Hungary, written by Brouska Hynek, titled "Slovakoj kaj Magiaroj", was ostentatiously presented to Alajos Aerenthal, Foreign Minister to the Austro-Hungarian Monarchy. Even foreign journalists and authors, like the British Seaton Watson, began to fashion their works in support of the Pan-Slavic cause. Watson's book, the "Racial problems in Hungary", became a primary source of anti-Hungarian propaganda for the nationalistically minded Slovak minority. Orchestrated under the direction of Hurban, Vajansky and Srobar, Watson received research information for his book only from Slovak sources. As a result, the book succeeded to undermine Hungary's chances for a just and lasting peace for many decades to come.

In this overheated atmosphere the reconciliatory attempts were bound to fail. The proposition of Csavolszky was put aside and the peace--plan of Gyula Just was hastily rejected by the pro-Czech Slovak politicians. Conciliation gave away to confrontation as in the spring of 1912, when the Slovak minority of Turócszentmárton (Martin) asked for the renewal of their "Slovenska Matica" charter, the Hungarian authorities because of imagined and real grievances, Srobar and Hlinka quickly assumed the leadership of the Slovak minority movement. The demonstrations, conferences, youth meetings of the time leading to the First World War created close links among the "realists" of Masaryk, the "socialists" of Srobar and the Czech and Slovak Catholic People's Parties. Such was the Slovak nationalists' movement when the war broke out. The Slovak socialists and democrats collaborated with the Czech manipulators. They all participated in the 1914 Congress at St. Petersburg and the Czech-Slovak Declaration at Moscow. Finally, behind closed doors. at the Pan-Slav Congress at Prague, the destruction of the Monarchy was decided.

CHAPTER 5

Minority Laws

The Sovereign Government of Hungary in the last phases of its functionality, when it was still possible to salvage the cause of freedom, ordered the debate on the Bertalan Szemere proposed Minority Bill. In early 1849, after the readings of the bill, the debate was postponed due to military developments. However, with the surrender of Serbia and a tentative Rumanian alliance signed, the government was hopeful and the managing of its internal affairs continued.

The Minority Rights Bill[18], which was a unique and significant effort to solve the problem of the minorities was passed into law on July 28, 1849, at the Szeged sitting of Parliamentary. The final text of the Minority Rights legislation read as follows:

"The rights of minorities within the boundaries of Hungary shall be ensured by the following decrees:

1. The official language of the government, administration, legislation and the military will be Hungarian.

In regard to the other languages used in the country, the regulations are as follows:

2. In municipal meetings every speaker may use his or her mother tongue; the language of minutes of the meeting is to be determined by the majority.

3. In county meetings everyone can use his or her own language. In the counties where the non-Hungarians are in the majority, the minutes of the meeting should be written in their language if the attendants vote for it. Correspondence with the government and other authorities shall be in Hungarian.

4.   At the common juries and courts, when the procedure is oral, the regulation of 3) will applies.

5.   The language of command in the national guard will be the same as the language of administration.

6.   In elementary schools, the teachers are to use the language of the community or that of the Church.

7.   The language of the register of birth, marriage and death and the Ecclesiastic affairs will be that of the Church.

8.   Applications to the authorities can be in any language.

9.   The annual council of the Orthodox Church is assured of free decisions in their religious and educational affairs. It can choose its bishops without outside influence or interference. It has the right to decide whether the Serbian and Rumanian Orthodox Church should be separated or remain united.

10.   The Orthodox Churches and their schools will enjoy the same advantages as the other churches and schools.

11.   The Orthodox churches will enjoy autonomy in their Ecclesiastical and educational institutes.

12.   A faculty of theology will be established at the University of Budapest, for the members of the Orthodox church.

13.   Appointments to all offices will be made on the basis of ability and merit, regardless of nationality and religion.

14.   The government is obligated to respect and put in practice the above principles and regulations.

15.   The government is authorized and expected to hear the wishes of Serbians and Rumanians and to remedy their grievances, either by its own power or through legislation.

16.   Finally, the government is authorized to grant amnesty to all who lay down their arms within the time determined and profess loyalty to the state."

The enforcement of the law was prevented by the surrender of Hungary at Vilagos on Aug. 12, 1849. The capitulation signalled the end of the first Democratic Government of Hungary and ultimately the loss of Hungarian sovereignty. With the collapse, the solution of the minority question was also laid to ruin. The advocates of the "Danubian Peace Plan" were silenced.

CHAPTER 6

The Idea of Federation

The Hungarian Ambassador to France, Count László Teleki, in his 1849 Spring[19] letters to the Hungarian soldier-statesmen, Kossuth, called his attention to the idea of a federation. Lajos Kossuth[20], who was also a principal figure in the 1848 independence campaign, was deeply concerned and committed to his nation's unity. He often pondered Hungary's minority problems and the question of autonomy Kossuth's plan[21] for a federation finally crystallised in 1851. His 'Great Hungarian Plan', as it became known, was dispatched from Paris to Hungary the same year. Unfortunately, Kossuth's detailed plan, which was to have been delivered and publicized by the representatives of the East Transylvanian Mack[22] and the Noszlopy movement[23] never reached the public.

Outside of the revolutionary council, the plan did not receive public scrutiny because between 1852 and 1854, most leaders of the freedom movement were disposed of by the administrators of the Austrian Empire. The Hungarian public was further kept in ignorance of the Kossuth Plan, by the undermining work of Károly Eötvös, Zsigmond Kemény and the aristocrats serving the Vienna court. This ignorance resulted in a lack of public support for the Kossuth federation concept, which had a grave bearing on the later developments. The idea of federation, which was accepted by the first democratically elected parliament of 1849, was neglected in the 1861 conferences, because of Vienna and her supporters. Due to public ignorance and Habsburg influence, the historic constitutional argument of the Austrian Monarchists prevailed.

The misunderstanding between Kossuth and the contemporary Hungarian society first occurred not in 1862, the year of the second version of his federative plan was released, but more than a decade before when his federative policy was substituted for his plan to grant equal rights to the minorities failed to materialize. Kossuth was clear by the early 1850's that the minority problems could only be saved by the formation of a Danubian Federation. The pragmatic historians of Hungary failed to point out that at the 1861 parliamentary session, which rejected the idea of a federation, the real problem was the lack of opposition rather than the formal disagreement between the parties of Ferenc Deák and Kálmán Tisza. The implementation of a Kossuth type federation would have led Hungary out of its political difficulties. Unfortunately, the only two politicians with any clear insight in this period were silenced. The one, Kossuth, was reduced to an idle spectator at Turin after the Prussian interference in 1854 and the death of Count Camillo Benso di Cavour in 1861. The other visionary, László Teleki, preferred to die rather than to give his name to an badly casted opposition party under the leadership of Prime Minister Tisza.

The minority problems surfaced again in 1861 but, sadly, the concerns were not treated in the same light as the principles arrived at in 1849. The minorities bound by the ideological shackles of "political nationhood", made any realistic solution almost an impossibility. The defeat of the Democratic Hungarian Independence Movement was also felt by the minorities. They too had to share the new wave of imperialistic oppression. All power was assumed by the Austrian authorities. The 'soldier barons', Kellesperg in Zagreb and Wohlgemuth in Transylvania, refused to hear of minority rights. Mayerhoffer, the "Landesschef" of Vojvodina, proclaimed Martial Law to suppress the rightful discontent in the recently created Serbian Volvodship. And so, it was absolute dictatorship, government without constitution, for over ten years. Instead of concrete directives, the Royal Diploma (Declaration) of October 20th, 1860, made vague promises. It suggested the convening of a Transylvania Congress but only in the presence of the Imperial Council. The Congress representatives, assembled from the minorities and subject nations, were to settle the interior affairs of the Serbian Vojvodship with the guidance of the council. The Imperial Patent (Command) that followed on February 26, 1861, contained even less substance for the minorities.

The Patent elicited wide ranging criticisms and reactions from the subjugated peoples. Among the Hungarians, it marked the beginning of active popular resistance, while the other minorities insisted on a "status quo" in order to ensure a certain degree of autonomy. Pan-Slav feelings prevailed even in the period of heartless arbitration, which should have brought all the minorities and subjugated nations closer together. The anti-Hungarian attitude of the minorities soon alienated the Hungarian leadership from the Slavs. Believing, that antagonism of such magnitude could only be the result of foreign instigation, the Hungarian popular mood was deeply and negatively effected by it.

Kossuth's negotiations abroad, however, had considerable effect on the formation of a reconciliatory climate. His views on the minority problems had crystallized during his forced emigration, between 1850 and 1860, and he became convinced that the future of all the peoples along the Danube could only be secured by the federation of the states. A Danubian Federation would neutralize if not eradicate the antagonism between nationalities and their minorities.

The development of the Kossuth Federation Plan and the Kossuth Minority Plan for the Hungarian territories are two separate issues. This book focuses on the plan and the minority question as it concerns Northern Hungary. After 1850, there were three specific proposals made by Kossuth and the Hungarian National Directorate. The first was in 1854, then 1859 and finally in 1860. The proposals were to address minority concerns and to find mutual political and social ground for conciliation. The first proposal made to Prince Obrenovic in London, in 1854, and published later in 1880 under the title of "Iratok" (Memoirs) in Budapest, Kossuth wrote:

> "We are willing to go to great lengths in our concessions, provided that the territorial integrity and political unity of our country will not suffer. I communicated this view of ours to the Prince and he found it perfectly satisfactory. He promised to support it by all means at his disposal and assured me of its approval."

In London, Kossuth and Obrenovic, the Hungarian and Serbian exiles, came to an agreement over minority and federative policies. Obrenovic's adept diplomat, Jovan Ristic, in his memoirs vividly

41

recalls that Mihály Obrenovic sacrificed much time and energy to build on the London agreement. And twice Obrenovic had to remind the Hungarian politicians that his administration supported and agreed in principal with the Kossuth Plan. The first reminder came, in March of 1861, when the Serbian Prime Minister, Garasanin and Ristic conferred with Vay, the chancellor of Austria, in Vienna, and shortly after with Andrássy and Eötvös in Budapest. The second time it was in the Spring of 1868, when Ristic called on Andrássy to remind the Hungarian Minister of the promise he made to Obrenovic in 1861, regarding the restructuring of counties along minority population lines. However, by this second time, Andrássy had reconsider the idea as impractical. The Obrenovic diplomatic overture would have helped to put in practice the law enacted by parliament on November 30th, 1868; (Act LXIV). This legislature was designed to uphold minority rights thereby disarming minority discontent and bringing an end to the passivity era. With the sudden death of Obrenovic, the friendly ties with the Serbians and the endeavour towards a federation were lost.

The details of the above negotiations are notable and relevant, because these events form the backdrop to the constantly shifting political landscape of the period. The sequence of events unfolded as follows; The conference of 1861 in Budapest was fruitless. In January 1868 Garasanin, Prime Minister of Serbia, entered into negotiations with the Bulgarian National Committee for propaganda, to promote cooperation between the two countries. In March, Garasanin came to a preliminary agreement with Nikita, the head of Montenegro, with respect to a Southern Slav Federation. In the meantime, a Serbian-Rumanian pact was being prepared, in order to "protect the Balkan sphere of interest". Later that April, Garasanin, requested Strossmayer, Bishop of Zagreb, to act as intermediary. in extending an invitation to the Croatians to join the South-East European Federation. The Charter of the Serbian-Bulgarian alliance was born in Bucharest in May, between the Serbian government and the Bulgarian Propaganda Committee in exile. At the same time, Obrenovic instructed Garasanin to establish contact with the government of Greece, to work out an agreement for the protection of the Greek and South-East European interests. Obrenovic repeatedly attempted to bring about a reconciliation between Hungarians and Serbians. Only when he failed to find on open door in Budapest, due to Austrian pressures, did he initiate negotiations for a South-East Federation. Then Obrenovic became the victim of a plot hatched in Vienna.

The second proposal of the Kossuth program dealt with policy recommendation towards the minorities. After the Serb-Hungarian Conference in London, the second proposal in collaboration with the representatives of the Hungarian National Directorate was dispatched on Jun 22, 1859 in a letter to the Nation. The dispatch contained the message of Kossuth, Klapka and Teleki and read as follows:

> "Like religion, culture is an all important factor in the life of a society. The state should do nothing to hinder these. Since the constitution guarantees it, the citizens have the right to create clubs and associations to defend their cultural identity. The laws are to be proclaimed in all the languages of its subjects."

The Hungarian National Directorate in September 1860 directed the third proposal to Cuza[24], ruler of Romania. This dispatch, which proposed civil, cultural, linguistic and religious rights for the minorities under the umbrella of nationhood, became known as the "Turin Memorandum". As Cuza was not interested, the plan received very little publicity in the Balkans. However, when Hungary's Minority Policy was about to be legislate, as a reminder to the members of the 24-29 Nov, 1868, Parliamentary Nationality Debates, the third policy proposal did receive publication in a Bucharest papers called the "L'Etoile D'Orient". As a result, Kossuth's policy in its final matured form was incorporated into the 1868 Parliamentary Bill. The legislature read in part as follows:

> "The equality of the cultural minorities and their languages were already accepted in principle by the Hungarian Parliament of 1849. This proposal only contains those clauses on which we all agree:

1.   Every community determines its own official language. The language will be used in its minutes of meetings, reports and letters to the government and the Parliament. It will determine the language of use in its schools.

2.   Every community will determine, by plebescite, the language of its administration. This language will be used in its records and documents, its correspondence with the government and also in the replies of the government.

3.   Members of the Parliament may use any language in the debates.

4.   The laws are to be proclaimed in all the accepted languages of the country.

5.   All Hungarian citizens have the right to gather, to form or join associations and to convene congresses, in order to safeguard their cultural rights and privileges.

6.   All minorities will enjoy autonomy in their ecclesiastical and educational affairs.

7.   All minorities have the right to set up the rules for their associations, cultural or religions.

8.   The state insists only on, that their meetings, records and documents should always be public. "

This policy proposal was the final outcome of the wide spread concern to settle the Hungarian minority questions. And in 1861, the ideological struggle became the politics of the day. Demands of the minorities were voiced one after the other. The situation led to the first reading of the Minority Bill mentioned above (1868, XLIV. article) and signalled the beginning of the reform era.

The April 2, 1861, Hungarian parliamentary session was to debate the constitutional position of the nation, with respect to the ruler of Austria and the minorities question. Ferenc Deák's two memoranda on the Hungarian Constitution was accepted by Parliament as the basis for any future constitutional debate. These memoranda, outstanding examples of constitutional literature, demanded the restoration of the Hungarian Constitution, on the basis of the Law that was in force in 1848. Obviously, this was a direct challenge to the Emperor's Imperial Unity principle, as issued in "October Diploma" of 1860, and reaffirmed in the 1861 "February Patent". Consequently, on August 22, 1861, Vienna dissolved the Hungarian Parliament.

The 1861 parliamentary debate was not to be forgotten, though. It resulted in political gains later. Unfortunately, the importance of the constitutional question and the Deák memoranda was overshadowed by the social reorganization question, during the debates. The Kossuth program was dropped from discussion. Although the minority question emerged several times during the debate, it was eventually pushed into to the background and no firm and binding decision ever came of it.

CHAPTER 7

Policies Towards the Minorities

Instead of a binding settlement, there was a kind of conciliatory policy toward the minorities of Hungary. Even this conciliatory mood gradually deteriorated between 1860 and the beginning of the First World War. Publicly the Tisza-Trefort-Andrássy triad recommended reconciliation, however, later developments displayed their lack of sincerity. In 1861 it was the nameless new politicians, László Szalay, Lajos Mocsáry, Virgil Szilágyi, Alajos Wlád, János Missic and Zsigmond Popovics, who represented the spirit of conciliation upon which lasting peace could have been built. Their comments called attention to the lessons learned during the 1848 revolution and the period of autocracy. The lesson learned was that, "the peoples of Hungary are interdependent". Deák[25] himself realized and stated as much in his first parliamentary proposal, that the cultural misunderstandings had to be cleared up and the lawful rights of the minorities had to be settled.

The minority question, which has stalled for some time, because of political neglect, was once again on the floor of the 1868 Parliament. Endre Medán, a Rumanian representative and Member of Parliament, participating in the Hungarian-Croatian negotiations, placed a motion before the House. He requested, that the February 1867 Serbian proposed Minorities Bill on the status of minority rights, be tabled once again as an agenda item for debate. The Serbian Minorities Bill, already introduced the previous year as a counter to the National Directorate's Minority Rights Bill, was radically different and challenged the one nation concept of the ruling party. Comparing the two 1867 parliamentary proposals, it becomes clear that the National Directorate's National Equality Bill[26] was designed to provided individual and cultural rights to citizens, regardless of language, cultural or religious affiliations, while the Medán's Serbian Minorities Bill[27] amounted to a declaration of independence for the minorities, guaranteeing cultural and political autonomy. It surpassed the Wlad Popovics plan of 1861, which spoke of one "political nation", where all citizens enjoyed equal rights. Medán's re-introduced Serbian proposal advocated national autonomy for the minorities, rather than promoting equality rights for all individuals, before the law. The full realization of the Serbian minority demands would have created a state within a state, where individual states could practice virtual self-government. In other words, a 'federation of states', loosely united under a new multi framed constitution.

The members of the 1868 National Directorate charged with drafting the new legislation were unable to bridge the conceptual gap of nationhood verses federation. Due to a deadlock, the 1868 legislative draft was substantially an unchanged version of the 1867 National Directorate proposal. Nineteen of the articles were nearly identical, four had stylistic modifications, and only five had changes worthy of mention.

Shortly prior to the 1868 National Directorate's legislative submission, Eötvös, the Minister of Education, on June 23 presented his legislative proposal. The Eötvös bill was tabled and debated the same year under article (1868: XXXVIII). Two clauses of this bill dealt with the education of the minorities. Paragraph 57 stated that religious education in the public schools shall be under the aegis of the ecclesiastic authorities. And, Paragraph 58 recognized the right of a citizen to be taught in his or her mother tongue:

> "Every pupil shall be taught in its own language, if
> it is one of the languages spoken in the community.
> Therefore the teachers hired should speak the
> languages of the community."

On the 4th of December, 1868, when the Eötvös bill was presented in detail and debate in the Upper House, only Samuel Masirievics, Serbian patriarch, found it unsatisfactory. In his view, the restrictions that were not necessitated by the basic principles of government and the unity of the Country, should be eliminated. Another member, László Wenckheim, criticised it for a different reason. Wenckheim's opinion was that the minority problems could not be solved simply by legislation. Some representatives of the Upper House considered the Eötvös-Deák proposal as a "revolutionary innovation". Somewhat reluctantly, Parliament did pass the National Equality Bill into law, and the law received Regal approval on December 7, 1868[28].

The National Equality Bill was built on three principles. First, the doctrine of political nationhood is a fundamental one. From this follows the second principle: cultural equality within the framework of the one nationhood concept, guaranteeing minority equal rights before the courts, in schools, ecclesiastical and cultural affairs. The third principle also flows from the first and is manifested in a liberal outlook and the protection of individual freedoms. To give expression to these principles, the bill was formulated in three parts. The introduction defined the concept of a "political nation" and argued that the language of national legislation must be the language of the majority, which is Hungarian. Next, the principle of minority equality and its implications were expounded and clarified in greater detail. Finally, the remainder of the bill was devoted to the legal protection of individual rights.

The tone of the Parliamentary debates, however, did not correspond to the actual national situation and its minority requirements. And while the National-Ecclesiastical framework, progressively got changed into a National-Political one, individual aspirations found a collective voice in the pursuit of liberal nationalism, with the aim of acquiring power. Ferenc Deák did not philosophize like Eötvös, did not set up a system, did not analyze the nationality question on a global scale, nor did he venture into prophecies about the future of the minority movements. He was a realist, thinking along constitutional lines, acclimatized to the compromise of 1867. Deák was not aware of the social fermentation and the class struggle around him. He thought that the political equilibrium restored by the Compromise necessitated the emphasis on a unified political nation, in opposition to the national aspirations of the minorities. Two great, selfless thinkers of the age, Deák and Eötvös prevailed over the requisites of their time. While the rights of the individual were guaranteed by the state, the ambitions of the minorities were unfulfilled.

Records indicate that the nationalistic ideas of the 19th century increased in strength after 1848. They assumed various forms. Among the Slovaks, there was a cultural-political movement led by the "Matica Slovenska". The Serbians demanded freedom of the press. The Rumanian Parliamentary Club and the Rumanian National Party, founded in 1867, launched a political movement to improve the lot of Rumanians in Hungary. Zsigmond Kemény, a well-known novelist and thinker of his age, warned the Hungarians:

> "Let us follow the advice of Széchényi given in 1842 and rejected by the public with indignation. Let us not condemn the zeal of other nationalities, the same zeal that has moved us to defend our great treasure, our mother tongue. The fire that roused Kazinczy, should it be denied to Kollár? Why should it not inflame the poets of the Slovaks and the Serbians? We Hungarians should refrain from the imposition of our language by aggressive means."

The conservative Kemény, the prophet, predicted the era of temptation which was to come. This should have been the time for understanding, moderation and solidarity among the Danubian nations. Dr. Lajos Mocsáry, perhaps the only person who could have reconciled the concept of political nationhood and the stand of the moderate representatives of the minorities, was not present when the National Equality Bill became law. The liberal doctrine of the political nation was gradually degenerating into power politics, through the effort of those who saw the minority question as an obstacle and a burden to national unity, precluding the possibility of a federation of the Carpathian nations.

The comparative linguist, Paul Hunfalvy, was also right when he pointed out that the mixed population of the United States was governed by the Anglo-Saxons, that there was an Irish problem in Great Britain and a Polish problem in the divided Poland, and with the exception of Switzerland, the minority problem was not solved anywhere, and this was a symptom of the age. The 1868 National Equality law lacked the instrument for its execution. The concept "political nationhood" was easily exploited to the detriment of the economic health of the Carpathian nations. In 1868 an opportunity was lost. Miletic commented, that "Hungary is the Gordian knot of Europe, cut by the Danube" may well have been justified.

CHAPTER 8

Passivity

After the proclamation of the 1868 National Equality Law, a new era began in the history of the Hungarian minorities. It was called the era of 'Passivity' by political writers of the period, because the minorities retreated into a state of passive and non-cooperative resistance in the face of the centralized power of the state. Andrej Mraz, a Slovak literary historian, in a study of post First World War Slovak novels, casting a retrospective glance on the Slovak literary contribution before the war, found that the writers and publicists of the period were content only to record their "grievances". High literary aspirations were nurtured by only a few.

The grievances of the minorities, whether actual or imagined, preoccupied almost exclusively the Slovak intellectuals of that period. The situation was no different among the Serbian and Rumanian populations of the country. There was a clash of interests. One of the primary reasons for the retreat of the intellectuals was the development of a dualistic system in Hungary, which caused a certain setback in the cultural and economic life of the minorities. In the economic and political rivalry of the liberal era the minorities lost their contact with the Hungarian middle class. Pest was no longer the mediator in the cultural disputes of the various class and cultural elements. And because of this class and cultural fragmentation, writers, publicists and politicians were drawn in different directions and the sense of belonging was weakening in the minorities.

Near the border areas, passivity was hardly felt at first. The educational directives of the National Equality law did not take effect until 1879 and therefore areas of mixed population did not experience immediate disturbance in their way of life. For the moment, minorities saw their cultural achievements as more significant than their political ambitious. This was clearly exemplified by the cultural works of the Serbian "Matica" at Ujvidék (Novy Sad), the Slovak "Matica" at Turócszentmárton (Martin) and the Transylvanian "Astra".

The minority passivity movement did not evolve just overnight. The Hungarian Parliamentary journals and minutes, between 1869 and 1872, are filled with busy schedules and the texts of many spirited debates between parliamentarians, especially those of the minority representatives. Even the 1868 "radicals" actively participated in all parliamentary activities. Miletic, for example, who had walked out of the House with many other in 1868, was busy during this period, speaking, proposing, interpellating. Vilmos Paulini-Toth, the president of the Turócszentmárton Matica, participated in national affairs discussions and demanded a say in national matters.

The new era was ushered in by the Serbians announcing of their political minority program. The 1869 Nagybecskerek conference, which gave birth to the Serbian Nationality Party, also introduced a minorities program as the party's political platform[29]. The Serbian Nationality program, which has been neglected by historical studies, turned into one of the most important programs for the age of Dualism. The far sighted approach of the conference set the tone for future nationalistic alignments of the minorities. The party referred to the "political nation" in a tactful way, while it called itself the Serbian National Party, Their program was the first one to peacefully challenge the National Equality Law. Using democratic and parliamentary means the Serbian National Party aligned itself with the Iráni and Simonyi lead Hungarian opposition party to find national support for the minority cause. The Serbian program conceived at Becskerek was a pioneer achievement, because it was conceived in the spirit of liberal democracy using constitutionally accepted methods to advocate minority convictions. The program was more than just another political declaration. It determined the direction of the Serbian minority right up to the First World War. Designed by Miletic, Polit and Jasa Timic, it set the tone for decades to come.

CHAPTER 9

Slovak National Aspirations

The direction of the Slovak minority policy for some decades after the 1867 Compromise, was chiefly aimed at their cultural preservation. Their attention was essentially focussed on educational questions. The 1863 founded "Matica Slovenska" did indeed defend the interest of its people on the political plane by such men as, Moyses, the Bishop of Besztercebánya and Daxner, a Tiszolc lawyer and architect of the Slovak minority's 1861 Nationhood Program. However, the impact of their influence on the Matica was far less than what was attributed to the cultural organization by the Slovak county deputies and the minority malcontents advocating cultural intolerance. The Compromise period provided many with hope, in that a reconciliation between the Hungarians and the Slovaks could be achieved. The hiring of Slovaks to public offices, such as the nominations for deputy-sheriff of Francisci in Lipto county and Daxner for Gomor, and the granting of charter to the Association of Slovak Women, etc... were promising signs for the process of reconciliation.

Many assimilated Slovaks with opportunistic motives had other designs. To cause dissent, people like Pál Madocsányi, Member of Parliament from Rózsahegy (Ruzomberok), Mór Zmeskál from Alsókubin (Dolnykubin), and Flórián Rudnyánszky from Bars, agitated against the Slovaks in the Parliament. Such affronts acted as poison and slowly became absorbed in the general public's opinion. After 1880, there were strong Pan-Slav manifestations in the Slovak press. As a result, three Slovak high-schools were closed and the Turocszentmárton Matica charter was revoked by the Hungarian authorities. In retaliation, the Slovak intelligentsia turned on the government and the "odrodilocs" (Vajansky, a period writer labelled the assimilated Slovaks as "half-breeds"). The Matica leadership had foreseen the dangers as early as 1873, and sent a memorandum to Prime Minister Jozsef Szlávy outlining the position of the Matica and its members. It read,

"The members of the Slovenska Matica will never forget that their ancestors lived here since pre-historic times, sharing the good and bad fortunes of the country. The members of the Slovenska Matica are peace-loving men who know very well that violent measures bring suffering and misery, rendering the future uncertain. Therefore they will never support undemocratic practices. They will use peaceful, legal means in the pursuit of their objectives..."

"Whether this association has been an effective one, whether it has succeeded in its endeavour, this can be reviewed openly."

"In this disconsolate situation, our deepest conviction is that the mistrust of our Hungarian brothers is due to their anxiety over their future, has a soothing effect. This fear is groundless; our desire is to restore the old trust tempered by the common experiences of a millennium, and to find a modus vivendi satisfactory to Hungarians and Slovaks."

Thus spoke the leaders of the Slovenska Matica.

The fact that the Matica, under the cover of its cultural work, promoted Pan-Slav agitations, was not mentioned. As well, the "modus vivendi" was not formed until 1875. This, coupled with the National Equality Law a lasting peace between the two peoples was greatly hindered. Once again, both sides missed their opportunity for reconciliation.

The historically significant 'Pact of 1868' was the last real opportunity for the forces of reconciliation. Its text, which was published in the "Correspondence Slave" and in the Hungarian papers of the period, received little attention since Jászi wrote about it in 1912. The Pact tried to address the question of the minorities by giving particular attention to the Fundamentality part[30] of the 1867 Minority Bill. If the first section of the proposal is examined, one can see how the Hungarian politicians' adroit diplomatic language did justice to the moderate 1861 Wlád-Popovic plan, which accepted the Hungarian political one nationhood concept. The resulting law provided for radical changes in the field of education, in the spirit of political unity within the state. (The importance of educational freedom was duly acknowledged in article XXXVIII. of the 1868 law.)

The ruling class of the age of 'Dualism' did not Hungarianize in order to assimilate the minorities. This would have run against the liberal spirit of the age. The Hungarianization fever under Prime Minister Kálmán Tisza, with its slogans "Political State" and "National Education", was the result of social unrest. It did, at least temporarily, succeed in deferring the land reform, the question of emigration and the plans to protect the interest of the workers.

Between the 1848 war of independence and the 1867 compromise, there were two Hungarys. One was the geographical or actual Hungary, and the other Hungary was in the imagination of Kossuth and his fellow emigrants who, with extraordinary foresight, hoped for a federation of the peoples along the Danube. The negotiations of Kossuth, aiming at a multi-cultural confederation, showed admirable consistency. What Kossuth proclaimed toward the Croatians in 1851, he maintained in 1854 during his London meetings with Obrenovic and in 1859 with the Rumanian, Cuza. This consistency showed in his September 15, 1860, memorandum, which was published by the Hungarian National Directorate, and continued in his 1861 "Iasi Plan", which expanded on the "Danube Confederation" concept in greater detail.

After that the minority problems left the field of theory and invaded the field of politics, the passions flared up again and the Pan-Slav movement regained its strength. Newer and newer demands were made by the minorities. Preparatory discussions were followed by hastily conceived proposals, which were presented amid grave misunderstandings. Although Kossuth's Confederative Plan was favourably received by the moderate politicians of the various minorities, his proposal was never really acted upon. Had Kossuth's principles been adopted in those negotiations, the burning problems could have been solved and the sting would have been taken out of the Pan-Slav movement.

The Parliament, on November 24, finally tabled the first debate on the 1868 National Equity Bill. The House was crowded, and the atmosphere was tense. The first to speak was Ferenc Deák. He set the tone of the debate by emphasizing that Hungary was a "political nation". His introduction was as follows:

> "Our time is short. I do not want to waste it by making a long speech. My conviction is that Hungary is a political nation: it is unified and indivisible, its subjects have equal rights, regardless of what cultural minority they belong to. I also believe that the official use of the various languages should by limited and subordinated to the national interest. This was part of the constitution, there is nothing new. Hungary a unified state, its citizens enjoy equal rights. National affairs cannot be dealt with using other languages or several languages. The language of legislation must be Hungarian. The laws should be translated to the other languages for distribution among all the minorities."

The concept of Political Nationhood was identical with the concept of Statehood in France, with the slight difference that the former had a feudalistic by flavour. Deák's policy was aimed at the elimination of conflict. It did not occur to him that it might become the official policy of the Era of Dualism. The Hungarian nation, or rather the Hungarian people, did not want to dominate the minorities. They did not care for state politics, rather they desired a peaceful settlement and a lasting reconciliation among all cultures concerned. The parliamentary debate lasted five days. Among passionate speeches, Misic, the leader of the Serbian representatives, suggested that the legislation should be to put off because the public mood was not ripe enough. Had his advice and the mood of the Hungarian people been heeded, the long period of barren passivity and brooding over grievances could have been avoided. The ensuing bitterness became fuel for the renewed flare-up of Pan-Slavism, which bred "Czechoslovakianism".

After the proclamation of the National Equality Law, a new era began in the history of the Hungarian minorities. Historians have labelled it the period of passivity, indicating that a certain passive resistance developed by the minorities against the centralizing efforts of the government. Andrej Mraz, Slovak literary historian, wrote that before the First World War Slovak writers and journalists were content recording the facts, the circumstances and their grievances, keeping their comments and proofs in their desk drawers for eventual use. The policy of the Slovak minority was camouflaged after the 1867 compromise. Their Pan-Slav idealogy became cloaked by their cultural activities. Their political agitation was kept within their clubs, while their public involvement in everyday politics was limited to educational questions. But a cluster of intellectuals around the Matica Slovenska, led by István Moyses, Bishop of Besztercebánya (Banskabistrica), who was imbued with the ideals of the Pan-Slav movement, did protect the interest of their people on the political plane.

In the Vienna ruled Austro-Hungarian Empire, Hungary and her cultural minorities all suffered under the Habsburg yoke. Vienna knew that if the 1867 compromise between Austria and Hungary had not been successful and the Hungarian politicians, diplomats and aristocrats were alienated from the influences of Austria, the leaders and peoples of Hungary would have found a just and peaceful way to form a Danubian Confederation. This, the Austrian rulership could never tolerate.

FOOTNOTES:

(PART I)

7. Tököly-Popovics Száva - (1761-1842) was an Arad land owner. In 1785 he received his Doctorate in Law from University of Budapest. He was Deputy Clerk in the County of Csanád for a few years, and in 1792 he was appointed as Secretary to the Hungarian Chancellery. In 1800, at the time of the levy in mass of the nobility, he was appointed as the Commander of the Arad Regiment. In 1802 he excelled as a zealous defender of the constitution. In 1838 two great foundations are created by him. Both of them were intended to help the talented, poor Serbian youth. At the University of Budapest and became known as the "Tökölyanum". Over 700 Serbian young men studied with the help of this scholarships.

8. Sándor Rudnay - Archbishop of Esztergom published his declaration titled "Slavus Sum" (I am a Slav). His declaration was intended to mobilize priests of Slavik origin, whom in turn were to incite the Slavik minorities. The original text of this declaration can be found in the archives of the Esztergom archbishopric under the title of "Acta Strigoniensis, 1830".

9. The events of the year 1867, which is so important to Hungarians, can be summarized as follows:

February 3: An imperial order is issued to convoke a meeting in preparation of a compromise between Austria an Hungary.

February 6: The preparatory debate is ended. Belcredi, Prime Minister of the Empire, makes an attempt to forestall the deal. The attempt is frustrated by Beust, the imperial Minister of External Affairs and Count Gyula Andrássy.

February 7: The Emperor Ferenc Joseph dissolves Belcredi's government and entrusts Beust with forming a new one. Count Friedrich Ferdinand Beust (1809-1886) is the descendant of an old German family. In 1849 he is Minister of Education in Saxony, later Prime Minister. Having opposed the initiatives of Austria for a long time, he took the side of Austria in 1866. After having fled with his king, he settled in Austria and became Minister of foreign affairs in 1866. And now Prime Minister.

February 8: Beust and Deák come to an agreement in Vienna. The emperor intends to ask Deák to form the Hungarian government. But Deák declines and recommends Count Andrássy.

February 12: The future Ministers participate in the cabinet meetings in Vienna.

February 17: Gyula Andrássy's government is formed. The Minister of Education is Baron Jozsef Eötvös, the Minister of Finance Menyhert Lonyay, the Minister of Transportation Imre Miko, the Minister of Justice Boldizsár Horváth. Deák does not accept a portfolio.

April 10: The autonomy of the counties is restored.

May 22: Kossuth writes a letter to Deák, trenchantly criticizing the terms of the agreement (the Cassandra letter).

May 29: The parliament approves the terms of the agreement (1867: XII. article). The Austrian-Hungarian Monarchy is born. The 59. paragraph calls for a customs treaty and trade agreement between Austria and Hungary. (The XVII. article fulfils this obligation.) The parliament acknowledges that the military and financial affairs are common affairs. The XV article assumes a part of the Empire's debt. Transylvania becomes once again an organic part of Hungary.

June 8: Ferenc Joseph , Emperor of Austria, is crowned king of Hungary. Elizabeth, in becoming queen consort, receives a crown as well.

July 22: the old Czech party sends a memorandum to the Emperor in which it demands the recognition of the state of Bohemia.

10.   **Matica** - Slovak cultural club.

11.   **Jan Holly** - (1785-1849) was a Roman Catholic parish priest. His two best known works are the "Szvatopluk" (1833) and the "Cirillo-Methodiana" (1835), both exposes. He was imbued with Pan-Slav ideas.

12.   **Andris Sládkovic** - (1820-1871) originally Braxatoris, was an evangelical minister. His important works: "Detvan" (1853), "Szvatomartiniada" (1861) and "Count Mikulás Subic Zrinsky na Sihoti" (1899).

13.   **András Hlinka** - was born at Csernova in 1865. In 1889 he was ordained priest in the diocese of Szepes, and from 1895 he was parish priest at Rozsahegy. He played an important role in the detachment of Northern Hungary. After 1919 he was in the parliament of Prague, trying to form an opposition party. The Czechs convicted and confined him.

14.   **Lörinc János Srobár** - was born at Liszkova in 1867. In 1886 he was
expelled from his school because of his Pan-Slav orientation. Having graduated in
Bohemia, he went to a university and became a physician. In 1906 he was a candidate
in the colours of the Slovak people's Party, but was not elected. He was imprisoned in
Szeged for agitation. In 1919 he became a powerful member of the Slovak cabinet, in
1921 Minister of Education in the Czech cabinet. In 1922 he was professor at the
University of Pozsony (Prague).

15.   **Milán Hodza** - was born in 1878 in Szucsany. He studied laws but became
a journalist. In 1903 he started a Slovak weekly and engaged in politics. He ended up
in Prague as Minister of Agriculture.

16.   **Gábor Ugron** - was born in Marosvásárhely in 1880. He became County
Lord Lieutenant in 1906, then Member of Parliament in 1915, and Minister of Interior
Affairs in 1917.

17.   **Lajos Láng** - (1849-?) economist and politician, Member of Parliament. In
1903 he became Minister of Commerce, later University professor, and member of the
Hungarian Academy of Sciences, In 1911 he was awarded the title of Baron.

18.   **The Minority Rights Bill of 1849** - The proceedings and enactment into law
of this bill was fully detailed in the book, "Magyarország függetlenségi harcának története
1848-ban és 1849-ben" (The history of Hungary's struggle for freedom in 1848 and
1849), published in Geneva in 1865, and written by Mihály Horváth, the Education
Minister of the Hungarian Government, while in exile.

19.   **The Balcescu-Ghica Federation Plan** - for the South-East European states,
preceded the Kossuth Plan. The Balcescu-Ghica plan proposed a common parliament for
the Hungarians, Rumanians and Southern Slavs but failed to deal with the minority
questions. Balcescu, the historian, saw the large problems and was apparently reluctant
to go into details. In his work, written while in emigration (Istoric romanilor sub Mihail-
Voda-Viteazu), he discusses the transylvanian question. Let us quote one sentence:
> "In Transylvania the problem is not -- or should not be -- how to
> get rid of the other nationalities but rather how to bring
> reconciliation on the basis of equality, within the frames of a
> federation of states."

20.   **Louis (Lajos) Kossuth** - (1802-1894) son of a noble but poor family, became
a lawyer and as one of the principal figures in Hungary's revolutionary struggle for
independence from Austria was swept up by the movement. The young lawyer-soldier-
statesmen established himself early as leader and protector of the independence
movement, travelling to North America in 1851 to publicize the fait of Hungary and its
people and win support for its cause.

21. The Kossuth Administrative Plan was concerned with the question of proposed political autonomy on various levels. The design was formulated on individual, educational and ecclesiastical rights as explained in Kossuth's letter to Teleki.

"Individual rights:

(a)   The leaders of the municipality decide what language to use in their discussions, records and minutes. An individual will have the right to use his or her mother tongue when speaking at meetings and in written applications.

(b)   The same applies to counties.

(c)   The government is to accept petitions and applications in any language used in the country. The official language is Hungarian, but the laws and decrees should be promulgated in all languages used.

(d)   The language of legislation is Hungarian. The parliamentary representatives may form nationality groups. These groups should look after the translations before the promulgation of a new law or decree by the government.

Educational rights:

(a)   A community cannot be without schools. The language used in the schools is the official language of the community.

(b)   A minority group in a community has the right to open its won school and use its own language.

(c)   Every county must have a high school (or high schools) which shall use the official language of the county.

(d)   Separate high schools may be opened for other nationalities in which they may use their own language.

(e)   Several counties, if they want, may found a university and decide the language to be used.

(f)   In a national University there must be faculties for all languages used in the country.

(g)   The teachers in a community are appointed and paid by the community, those in a county by the county.

61

(h)   The state must provide for the required number of educational institutes for all nationalities.

Religious rights:

(a)   All religious and denominations will have equal rights.

(b)   The state will not interfere in ecclesiastic affairs. Every religious group will have a certain autonomy. However, a religious group cannot become "state within a state"."

This plan of Kossuth was further amplified in his treatise entitled "Characteristic features of the constitution of Hungary, with special regard to the solution of its minority problems". The remarks in the appendix of the 1851 constitutional proposal regarding Croatia, Transylvania and the Serbians are significantly supplemented. About Croatia, Slavonic and Dalmatia, Kossuth in his July 9,1852, New York address clearly stated that:

> "These peoples have always been separate and autonomous entities,
> I consider it just and fair to grant them independence as far as their
> interior affairs are concerned, an autonomy similar to that of the
> states of the U.S.A., retaining only the national defense, foreign
> relations, the customs and commerce and the control of the roads
> leading to the seas in the scope of the central government."

> "In order to ward off any mistrust" says Kossuth to the Croatians
> and Slavonians" on behalf of my people I solemnly tell you that the
> Hungarians have no desire for domination. All they want is to
> shake off the yoke of the Habsburgs, with the help of Croatians
> and Slavonians. Having achieved this, Hungary is willing to form
> alliances with these nations on the basis of equality, like the states
> of North America. Should they be ever tired of this bond, we are
> willing to recognize Croatia and Slovenia as completely
> independent neighbour state, with the only stipulation that Fiume
> should remain free to decide whether it wants to be an independent
> city of commerce or under the sovereignty of Hungary or Croatia."

Kossuth did not consider Transylvania a separate entity, so he did not offer special concessions to its nationalities.

The questions regarding the Rumanians and Saxons of Transylvania are not the subject of this study.

To the Serbians, Kossuth repeats his peaceful intentions in which he had assured Garasanin many times, emphasizing the basic principles of his plan:

"Our Serbian brothers and sisters are mingled with other races. They should not be dominated by others. And I presume they do not want to dominate others either. I tell you, with the sincerity of my brotherly feelings, if my fellow citizens of other nationalities have any desires I have not dealt with, it is because I am not aware of them. Be convinced that the Hungarian nation has forgotten all the mutual grievances of old, that it offers its hand and is willing to give anything that a brother can expect from a brother."

22. **Jozsef Mack** - (1810-1868) moved to Transylvania after the surrender at Világos, and was arrested and convicted for conspiracy. After his release in 1851 he fled to Kiutahia, Turkey. Later, allegedly commissioned by Kossuth, he returned to Transylvania and tried to organize another conspiracy. This was discovered too. He emigrated to the United States just in time. Died in Carolina.

23. **Gáspár Noszlopy** - (1820-1853) was a district administrator at Marcal before the 1848 revolution. In 1849 he became the commissioner and military commander of Somogy and Tolna. He recruited a troop of 3000 men and sent a full battalion of Komárom. After the capitulation of Komárom, he went into hiding in the Bakony Mountain, later he managed to escape to Kecskemét. In 1852 he wanted to capture Ferenc Joseph, the Emperor. He was seized, but managed to escape again for a few months. He was finally caught and hanged on March 3rd, 1853. Four of his companions were executed and some other were incarcerated.

24. **Sándor Cuza** - (1830-1873) studied in Paris, Pavia and Bologna. In 1848 he had to flee from the Russians and received refuge in Vienna. After the Russians left, he became the adjutant of Prince Sándor Vogorides (Pasha Aleko), a member of the Turkish council of state. After the resignation of Vogorides, Cuza became Turkey's Minister of War. On the 5th of February 1859, Moldavia and Havaselve made him Reigning Prince. Under him the two regions became united and named Rumania. His reign did not last long. Because of his absolutistic endeavour he was compelled to abdicate on the 22nd of February 1866.

25. **Ferenc Deák** - (1803-1876) Hungarian Statesmen, liberal politician. One of the Nineteen Century's greatest Hungarian political thinkers and historians, Deák became Justice Minister in the Batthyány Government of 1848. Instrumental in the 1867 Austro-Hungarian Compromise, he was dubbed as the "Wisdom of the Nation". He refused a ministerial portfolio in the Government following the Compromise, but remained the leader of the Deák Party. Once again he was instrumental in introducing and shaping the post Compromise National Equity and Minority Bills.

26.   **The National Equality Bill:**

The various nationalities within Hungary have equal rights in the use of their respective language. As for the principle of equality and its practical application in the fields of administration and jurisdiction, the following points will serve for clarification:

(1)   Every citizen has the right to use his or her own language in communications with the local authorities and in applications and petitions sent to the government. Correspondence with other municipalities should be done in the language (or one of the languages) of the recipient community. In the area of judicial matters the use of language is regulated in paragraphs 14-21.

(2)   In municipal and ecclesiastical meetings the speakers are free to use their mother tongue.

(3)   Every citizen, community or Church has a right to open schools, on all three levels, and other institutes for the promotion of art, science, economy, industry or commerce and set up regulations and rules for these institutes. The rules, however, must be approved by the government. And the management of the funds is to be supervised by the government. The institutes so created will have the same rights as similar institutes of the state, the one condition being that the schools curricular must be in harmony with the general rules. The language of private institutes or clubs is to be chosen by the founders.

(4)   The dioceses determine what language to use in dealing with ecclesiastic affairs, in their schools within the frames of school regulations.

(5)   Higher Church authorities may use their own language in their interactivities. But the minutes of their meetings are to be submitted to the Hungarian government.   Correspondencebetween the various Church authorities will be in Hungarian.

(6)   Petitions of Church authorities addressed to a government office will be bilingual or in Hungarian.

(7)   Cities, towns and villages choose their own language of communication. If 20% of the members consider it desirable to use another language in additions to the chosen one, the minutes of the meetings will be bilingual.

(8)   The clerks of a community must use the language of the community in their communications.

(9)   A community may use its own language in its correspondence with its own jurisdiction and with governmentofficers. In its correspondence with other jurisdiction, it is to use Hungarian or a language of the territory addressed.

(10)   The reports and the records of judicial institutes are to be in the language of the state. But additional languages, too, can be used if it is the wish of at least 20% of the members eligible to vote.

(11)   The clerks of judicial institutes will use the Hungarian language in their interactivities; but if this should bring invincible difficulty to any of the clerks, another language of the minutes may be used.

(12)   These clerks, in communications with citizens or associations in their own territory should use their language.

(13)   Local authorities in their correspondence with other localities and with government offices will use the state language (and additional languages if desired).

(14)   Every citizen who is before the court without a legalcounsel, whether as plaintiff or as defendant, whether in person or by a proxy.

    (a)   may use his or her mother tongue.

    (b)   in a court of another locality must use one of the accepted languages of the area.

    (c)   in his or her own county may use a language of his or her community.

    (d)   in courts elsewhere they must use a language in use in that part of the country.

(15)   The judge is to hear the plaintiff, defendant and witnesses in their own language. The recording is, however, done in Hungarian. Its contents should be explained, if necessary, through an interpreter. The judge is obliged to make sure that all the parties understand the contents of important documents as well. Summoning will be done in the mother tongue of the summoned or, at least, in an official language of that area. The decision or sentence of the judge or jury must be proclaimed int he state language, but also in the language of the parties concerned in so far as the language is one of the official ones used in that area of jurisdiction.

(16)   In case of an appeal to a higher court, the judge is obliged to have all documents translated to Hungarian and to submit these translations, with all records pertaining to the case, to the higher court. The decision or sentence of the higher court must be proclaimed in Hungarian and in the language of the parties involved. *(See paragraph (15))*

(17)   In trials and suits conducted with lawyers, the language used will be Hungarian. The only exception is the language of summons. Its is regulated in paragraph (15). Every party is obliged to submit non-Hungarian documents translated into Hungarian. Translation approved and accepted by both counsels will be considered valid. If, however, the validity of the translation is doubted, the service of an official translator will be used to determine its validity. For this purpose, competent translators will be employed wherever necessary, at the expense of the state. If a language cannot be handled by the translator at hand, the document will be submitted to the Ministry of Interior Affairs.

(18)   In commercial courts dealing with matters related to bills of exchange, the language will be that of the state.

(19)   The secular courts will use Hungarian in their internal dealings, the courts of the Churches are free to determine the language to be used.

(20)   The land registration offices shall use the state language. The decree, however, must be translated in to the language of the clients at their wish.

(21)   The primary language of the judicial and legal offices will be that of the state.

(22)   If petitions of private citizens, Church authorities or members of communities that do not have their own jurisdiction, are submitted in a language otherthe Hungarian, the government office must have its decision translated into the language of the applicant.

(23)   In the educational institutes founded by the state the language to be used will be determined by the Department of Education. This same department must assure that all the nationalities living in the country have enough pre-university schools that teach in their mother tongues.

(24)   In areas where more than one language is spoken, colleges should have faculties for each language.

(25)   In the state colleges and universities a faculty will be set up for each nationality that is heavily represented int he area.

(26)   In the foremost university of the state, the lectures will be in Hungarian; a faculty for each language used in the country should be set up.

(27)   Applicants for jobs shall be judged by their abilities and qualifications, regardless of their culture.

(28)   Laws of the past contrary to the above are declared void. Paul Sommsich, chairman of the committee. Lajos Horváth, convener of the committee.

27.   **The Serbian Minorities Bill:**

(1)   In Hungary, the Hungarian, Rumanians, Serbians, Slovaks, Russians and Germans are recognized as nationalities with equal rights whose political equality, within the frames of the state's territorial and political unity, is guaranteed by law. Every nationality may display its national flag, along with the Hungarian flag, in its public meetings and celebrations.

(2)   The representation of a nationality and the sphere of its language rights will reflect its size. The boundaries of counties and election districts will be adjusted in an attempt to give each area a certain unified character. A national committee will be formed without delay. Its task will be to study the situation in all parts of the country and after careful consideration to propose boundary adjustments wherever they are needed.

(3)   In a community, district or county, the language of the nationality in majority will be the language of public affairs, provided that nationality is one of the six mentioned above. In the case of mixed population, if the second strongest ethnic group (again provided it is one of the six) approximates the number of the one in majority, its representatives may demand that their own be accepted as second language. In areas where the nationality in majority is not one of the six, the official language will be the language of the county but the dominating ethnic group may use its own language in their local affairs.

(4)   All six nationalities should be well represented in the Upper House, in government offices, in high courts of justice, on the administrative boards of counties, in all branches of the government. The language of legislation and of the central government is Hungarian. But in local meetings and councils another language may be used. In the parliament the representatives of the various nationalities may speak in their own language.

(5)   The laws of the country and the decrees of the government are to be communicated with the six nationalities in their own languages. If there is any discrepancy between the original and the translated text the original must be considered correct and binding.

(6)   The administrators of counties, districts and towns, the district courts and lower courts may use their own language in their correspondence with the central administration and the government, and are to receive the decisions in the same language (with the exceptions mentioned in paragraph (5)). Two boroughs, if their language is the same, use their own; if not, their submissions must be bilingual: their own and the principal language of the state. This rule applies to villages as well, if its language is recognized. Otherwise these communities must use one of the languages prevalent in the county or district of the addressee.

(7)   On trials and hearings, the parties may use their own language and the decisions will be proclaimed in their language. If the language of the plaintiff or that of the defendant is not one of the privileged languages, he or she may use the language of the other party or the language of the state. If one of the parties consists of persons of different nationalities, they have to choose a language of one of their own, or else the official language. On trials of criminal courts the language of the accused is to be used throughout the whole procedure if it is one of the official languages in that district; otherwise one of the official languages the accused understands most. These rules apply to the interrogations of the witnesses as well.

(8)   Education is the responsibility of the state. Its promotion by grants and in other ways is one of the top priorities of the state. Every nationality has the right to set up organizations, schools and institutes for the cultivation of science, literature and art and operate them as they please. For these purposes they will need government grants that should be made available through their representatives in the parliament and government departments. In those branches of education which overlap the field of religion, the government and the Churches will jointly determine the rules to be followed.

(9)   In the schools of the six nationalities referred to above the language used in teaching is their own. Their educational institutes will have the same rights as the national institutes as long as their curricula are kept in harmony with the state curricula. Wherever the subject of history is included, besides the history of Hungary their own history is to be taught. The Churches and educational institutes, as well as the institutes mentioned in paragraph (8). may use their own language in their communications and expect replies in the same.

(10)   In the leading university of the state, besides the chairs of language and literature for the six nationalities named above, there will be chairs for the study of laws in the languages of the nationalities. This applies to academies of law as well wherever there are enough non-Hungarians to justify it. In areas where there are no schools for the ethnic groups living there, the government will help them to open schools.

(11)   The fundamental principles of this law contained in paragraphs 1 and 2 flow from the spirit of the constitution.

(12)   All previous laws contrary to this one are declared void. The signatures: István Branovacsky, the representative of Ujvidék, Jozsef Hodosiu a representative of Brád in the county of Zaránd, Zsigmond Borlea, deputy of Rittberg in the county of Temes, Endre Medán, repr. of Remete, Gergely Pap, dep. of sz. cseh of the C. of Knlso-Szolnok, János Popovics Dessenan, repr. of Mariaradua in the C. of Arad, Pal Trifunácz, repr. of Basahíd, Demeter Jonescu, repr. of Nagybécskerék, Sándor Románn (Alexandrn Roman), repr. of Cseke in the C. of Bihar, Antal Mocsonyi, repr. of Bilages in the C. of Arad, Vince Babesin, repr. of Szászkabány in the C. of Krasso, Florian Varga, repr. of Szt.Anna int he C. of Arad, Zsigmond Popovics, repr. of Butyin in the C. of Arad, Dr. Szvetozar Miletic, repr. of O-veise, Emil Manojlovic, repr. of Vérsed, Miklos Dimitrijevic, repr. of Kulpin, György Mocsouji, repr. of Moravica in the C. of Temes, Péter Csermovics, Zsigmond Papp, Szvetozar Millutinovic, repr. of Tovarisova in the C. of Bács.

28.   The National Equality Law (1868 XLIV Law):

Since all the citizens of Hungary belong to one political state, in accordance with the basic principles of the Constitution; and since this equality admits regulations only in the use of the various languages and only in sofar as the unity of the state, the practicality of its administration and its jurisdictional system necessitate; The following will serve as guide lines for the use of the different languages:

(1)   As the official language of the state is Hungarian, the parliamentary debates will be, like it has been, in Hungarian. The laws, however, are to be promulgated in the languages of all nationalities found in the country. The langauge of the government in all its branches will be Hungarian.

(2)   The records of municipalities and district or county boards will be in Hungarian, also in any additional language requested by at least 20% of the board members. In case of a discrepancy the Hungarian original is to be considered valid.

(3)   In meetings of the administrators everyone having the right to speak may use his or her mother tongue.

(4)   Local authorities use the Hungarian language in their correspondence with the central government. Among themselves they can use Hungarian or else a language in use by the board or office addressed.

(5)   In dealing with their own affairs, local authorities should use Hungarian. Exceptions can be made, though. But the reports and the related documents should be submitted in Hungarian as well if the nature of the matter requires it.

(6)   The local authorities, in their communication with institutes, clubs or private persons in their own area should use the language of the party addressed if possible.

(7)   In suits, if the service of a lawyer is not used, every citizen of the country (or his or her proxy)

(a)   may use his or her mother tongue in the court of his/her locality.

(b)   must use one of the official languages of the court outside his or her locality.

(8)   In the cases referred to in paragraph 7, the judge will hear the plaintiff or applicant in his or her language, the witnesses too but the records will be written in the language chosen by the parties in dispute or, if they cannot agree, in one of the official languages; in the latter case, their contents must be imparted to both parties through an interpreter. The judge has to have the related documents translated as well. The summons should be in the language of the summoned or else in the language used in meetings.

(9)   In criminal and civil courts, whenever the service of lawyers is used, the present rules are to be observed until the central authorities issue new instructions in accordance with the final decision arrived at in the legislative body.

(10)   The Church courts may use the language of their own choice.

(11)   The cadastral registries are to use the language of the law-court they are dealing with. But, if requested, the decision and the docket should be given in the language of the state or in one of the languages used in that area as well.

(12)   If a suit is conducted in a language other then Hungarian, and the case is forwarded to an appeal court, the records and documents are to be translated by the official translators of the appeal court, and Hungarian will

be used in the sessions. The decisions and sentences of a high court will always be proclaimed in Hungarian. These decisions, having been returned to the lower court, must be announced to each party in the language of their respective wish.

(13)   The language of all courts set up by the state will be Hungarian.

(14)   The dioceses determine the language they want to use in their internal affairs; and also the language used in their schools, provided this does not contradict a state law.

(15)   Higher Church authorities determine the language to use in their reports, records and correspondence with the dioceses. if this language is other than Hungarian, the records are to betranslated into Hungarian for the critical perusal of the government.

(16)   Churches may communicate with each other inHungarian or in the language of the addressed church.

(17)   High Church authorities may use Hungarian or their own language in their submissions to the government. In their communications with municipalities, either Hungarians or one of the languages accepted in that area. The dioceses use Hungarian or their own language in their contacts with the government or with the municipal authorities in their own territory; in their correspondence with other municipalities, their language.

(18)   In educational institutes founded by the state, the language of teaching will be decided by the Minister of Education, unless it is regulated by law. But it is the duty of the government to see to it that all the nationalities have the opportunity to learn in their mother tongues up to the academic level.

(19)   In those areas with strong minorities, high schools and colleges sponsored by the state should have chairs for their languages and literature.

(20)   In the highest university the language used is Hungarian. But every nationality will have its own chairs for language and literature.

(21)   The meetings in towns and villages may use the language of their choice; in their records one or more languages requested by at least 20% of the members.

29.   **The Serbian National Party's Political Platform:**

(1)   The Serbian representatives, together with the Rumanians, Slovaks and Ruthenians, shall promote the equality of all nationalities, in the spirit of the proposal made by the Serb and Rumanian deputies in the last session of the parliament. The Conference enjoins the Serb deputies to stand by the proposal mentioned and to have the parliament put the decisions of the 1861 Serb congress on its agenda and, should they suffer alterations or modification, to insist on convening a new Serbian national congress for the purpose of reconciliation. In any case, the deputies are asked to support whatever the Serbian people deems right and fair.

(2)   In the interest of the Serbo-Croatian nation living int he Ternary (Croat-Slovene-Dalmatian) kingdom, they shall support its autonomy, in accordance with the national Serbo-Croatian party.

(3)   They shall support the wish of the Rumanians: the territorial autonomy of Transylvania and the equality of all its peoples.

(4)   In the interest of the nationalities in Hungary, they shall attack the 1867 XII. article, i.e. the compromise between the Austrians and Hungarians, for its anti-Slav tone, and collaborate with the opposition party in the parliament. In legislation they should work for the democratization of counties and municipalities, for their autonomy. Let them demand freedom, individual, social and political, on the basis of principles acceptable in a constitutional, democratic state. Let them promote liberalism.

(5)   In the interest of our Slav kin beyond the river Lajta, they shall support them and their aspirations for equality and autonomy, without violating the constitution.

(6)   In the interest of the freedom of Christian peoples and the unity of the Eastern Serbs, all policies aiming at the preservation of Turkey (its status quo.) or at the occupation of Serbian territories, must be foiled. The Christian minorities within Turkey must be supported.

(7)   The Serb representatives appointed by the Serbian party should unite with the liberal Slovaks and Rumanians in one party and they should form a political club outside the parliament.

30.   **The Minority Bill:**

(1)   The following settled nationalities are found in Hungary: Hungarians, Rumanians, Serbs, Slovaks, Ruthenians and Germans,. All these

are equal before the law. This law defines the lingual and political equality of the above nationalities, with a view to maintaining the political unity of the state. In official documents, the expression "people of Hungary" comprises all the nationalities.

(2)   In the counties, towns and villages the nationality that is in the majority is considered dominant. In the counties and districts where a non-dominant nationality reaches one third of all the population, this second language may be considered the second official language. In meetings of the administrative body either language can be used. In districts where neither nationality is in the majority, any accepted language may be used but in correspondence with Hungarian authorities or with the government the official language of the county must be used.

(3)   In legislation and in documents of the central authorities the language to be used is that of the majority in the country. The central government, the high court of justice and the Court of Cassation must translate its directions and decrees into the dominant language of the county addressed. The representatives of minorities in the parliament may use their mother tongue.

(4)   The laws of the state, the decrees and orders of the government must be promulgate in all six languages.

(5)   The administrators of counties, districts and towns may communicate with higher authorities in their own language.

(6)   In ordinary and appeal court trials, the parties may use their own languages. In a suit, though both the plaintiff and the defendant may use his or her own language, the decision will be proclaimed in the language in which the case was submitted. If the language of one party is not understood in the locality, theopponent's language, the official language of the county or Hungarian may be used by that party. In case one party consists of several persons of different nationalities, one of official languages of the district must be used. The language used in a suit should be that of the defendant and the decision must be announced in the same provided it si one of the official languages of the district. It not, the language best understood by the defendant must be used. If there is more than one defendant and they belong to different nationalities, those who understand the official language of the district will be heard in that language and the others as well, with the help of an interpreter. The decision must be delivered in the language of each person involved.

(7)   The advance of its citizens is to be promoted by thestate. All nationalities have the right to open schools and found literary, art and science clubs and institutes.

(8)   The language of teaching in elementary and high school should be the language of the nationality in majority in that district. The government is obliged to inform the educational institutes of its decisions in the language of teaching.

(9)   In the universities the language and literature of the various nationalities will be taught and also chairs will be created for each nationality to acquaint the students with the laws of the country in their own language. Moreover, courses can be introduced for all branches of science in various languages. This applies to academies as well. In each district the nationality in majority will be favoured. In areas where there is no school, the state or municipality must open one without delay.

(10)   Everyone who wants to apply for a job which requires the knowledge of Hungarian must prove that he or she has mastered the language.

(11)   This law will be in force immediately after its approval and proclamation and previous laws contradicting it will be void.

PART II.

NORTHERN HUNGARY

CHAPTER 1

Opposing Historical Views

Where is the man whose daring lips
Can stir up the depths, blind and horrible,
And after centuries show us Árpád
In panther skin, and his people's fearful
    might?...

Becoming a State is a significant mile stone in the life of a people. It is a measure of its development. From a philosophic view of history, however, this is not quite true. Still, many believe that the only movers and determinants of history are the states, therefore the peoples that have not reached the stage of statehood, have no history in the real sense of the word. And if so, we should deem them inferior.

The statehood of a people is certainly an important factor, but not a decisive one. Historic studies based on archeological facts collaborate that prehistoric people, who never founded a state, in the modern sense, established communities and tribal structures, which resemble our modern state and that through their customs and laws undoubtedly shaped the future of mankind.

The positivistic view of history tends to disregard the essence of things and to deny the possibility of the cognizance of regularity. Our knowledge is determined by the limitations of our sensory perceptions. Relying only on the observed for input, virtually denies the validity of the thinking process. To the positivist, human knowledge is the sum of collected scientific data and nothing more. He cannot see the trustworthiness of deduction or inference.

The positivist view strongly influenced historians at the turn of the century. Flattery toward the reigning dynasty or loyalty towards the ruling class was, in certain cases, the main motivations. The result

77

was a distorted account of history. But worst. the bias that tainted the historical records also put its stamp on legislation. People identified state with nation and confused citizenship with nationality. A price was to be paid for this later. For example, since the dictated peace treaty of Trianon, Hungarians were deeply affected by the internationally created succession states of Czechoslovakia, Rumania and Yugoslavia, and their human rights violations against minorities within their borders. But, the most painful result of Trianon was not the loss of more than two thirds of her territory, but the enfeeblement of their self-respect.

A nation can be kept on its feet only through the awareness and the nurture of its tradition. The phenomenon of fading national consciousness is usually the fruit of distorted and falsified history. In such a climate, apathy is born, which may corrupt generations. This happened in Hungary while Czech, Slovak and Rumanian historians, attempted to rewrite history in their fashion, even in the face of long recorded and confirmed historical facts. The presence of the Hungarians in the Carpathian Basin has been a thorn in the side of the Pan-Slavic movement for the last two centuries. In their desire to unify all Slavs under one great empire, their willingness to subjugate or eliminate opposition from any source should raise international concern.

The true political history of Northern Hungary has not been written yet. But, there is a number of propaganda "documentations" published in the Czech, Slovak and German languages, and the French published Masaryk-Benes fabrications, which played a key role in the disfigurement of Hungary. The democratic structure of Northern Hungary was completely ignored by the persuaders and the persuaded. To Quote from the work of Gyula László, a Hungarian archeologist and historian:

> "After the death of Attila, the ruler of the Huns (453
> A.D.), we find Germanic people in the Carpathian
> Basin for a hundred years. They are practically
> wiped out by the armies of Charles the
> Great in 800.

The Franks take Trans-Danubia and the Bulgarian
Transylvania aboutthe same time. The Slavs begin to
appear in the ninth century. This is the situation in
896, the year of Árpád's conquest of Hungary, the
beginning of our millennium." [1]

The quest of this book is not to study the ancient history of the
Magyars, but rather to investigate Hungarian claims to their territory,
starting with Árpád's arrival at the Carpathian mountains. The
motivating force for their westward drive was the need to find a place,
which afforded natural protection and fertile land in order to support
population growth. The invasion of the Carpathian Basin took place in
perfect military order. As Jozsef Kovacsics in his book, "The historical
demography of Hungary"[2], writes that Árpád's people were divided
into 108 clans or tribes and numbered 20,000 soldiers amongst them.
The areas settled by the clans and divided along 50 dominant tribal
lines became the counties of Hungary.

When the Magyars arrived at the Carpathians, Moravia did not
exist. Swatopluk had been their ruler for 25 years, until 894. The
invasion occurred in 896. What should we make of Constantine's
account, which stated that the Moravian Empire was scattered by the
Magyars?[3] The conclusion that archeology and anthropology have
come to, independently, is that the Avars were far from extinction at
the end of the ninth century, nor were they absorbed by the Slav
culture. They spoke a language the new comers easily understood.
For they were Magyars too, in fact they were the precursors of Árpád's
people, who lived in that land since about 670 A.D. Archaeologically
rich findings from Szabolcs, and in particular Northern Hungary,
indicate that there is nothing of Slav origin among them. The names
on the grave stones, the villages, rivers and farm roads, all bear
testimony to Avar-Magyar tribal settlements in Northern Hungary.

CHAPTER 2

The Carpathian Basin

West of the line drawn between the Baltic Sea and the Black Sea is situated, what can be called, the interior of Europe. The culture, the economy and the social structure of the peoples living in this part of Europe have many common features. In the middle, embraced by the Carpathian Mountains, is the Carpathian Basin. Throughout history, this area was not just a meeting place, it was a point of collisions. Its geographic location, which determined much of its cultural and economic development, also provided the soil for conflicting political aspirations. Naturally, a great deal of intermingling took place here. The eastern and western influences are as obvious here as those of the North and South. In all this, for over a millennia, the dominant and determinant people of the whole area were the Hungarians.

Authors of contemporary geographic and political literature showed unusual preference in using the title Eastern Europe or South-Eastern Europe for this region instead of Central Europe, reserving the latter for the German settled areas. This misconception can largely be attributed to power politics and propaganda. Trying to align themselves with German interests, the Czechs considered themselves as Central Europeans as early as the end of the eighteen century. In Pan-Slavic terms, they saw themselves superior to the peoples South of their country and referred to them as South-Easterners.

Politically as well as geographically up to the nineteen twenties, the Carpathian Basin was considered to occupy a central position among the European states. Recent geopolitical studies testify to its centralist character. The geopoliticians of the French "Larousse Encyclopedia"[4] and of the German "Kritik aus Zentral Europa"[5] affirm the centrality of the Carpathian Basin. Besides location and the natural conditions, there are human factors, of course, that contribute

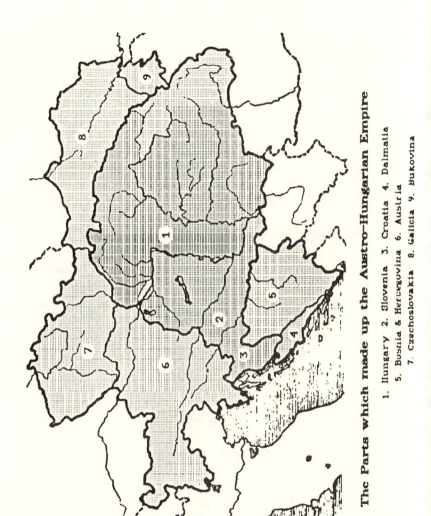

The Parts which made up the Austro-Hungarian Empire

1. Hungary 2. Slovenia 3. Croatia 4. Dalmatia
5. Bosnia & Herceguvina 6. Austria
7. Czechoslovakia 8. Galicia 9. Bukovina

to shaping the life of people. The territory that should be properly called Central Europe has seen, in the course of centuries, remarkable changes reflecting the cultural stirs caused by occasional migrations. As the population, was more and more drawn to agriculture and settle down, the focal point of culture exerted greater influence on larger areas and the economic and political position of Central Europe took a definite direction.

Historically, around the tenth century, the Carpathian Basin was obviously near the eastern boundary of Europe. In time, as the state of Poland extended, the edge of the European continent began to shift towards the East. By the sixteenth century, this shift caused the Carpathians to be in the centre of Europe. And today, the Carpathians are considered as the dividing line between the West and East European culture and civilization.

In Hungary, West-European life style, architectural styles and religions meet with South-European ways, sentiments and tastes. It is considered, that a fair measure of general education level of an area is the number of literates among the people. In this respect, the southern and eastern range of the Carpathians and the river Száva constitute a clear dividing line. For example, in the region South of the river Száva, the proportion of literacy among the population is over fifty percent, whereas North of the Száva river, it is only ten percent. Toward the East the situation is only slightly better. Within the Carpathians, one finds a lower level of education among the Slovaks, Rumanians and Ruthenians who inhabit the mountain areas. However, this literacy level is far above that of the country of Rumania.

The distribution of languages and religions attests to the central position of the Carpathian Basin. All three great language families, the Germanic, Slav and Rumanian, reach into this territory. None of them, however, have become a dominant language in the area for it was Hungarian, ever since the tenth century which dominated this central region. Intermingling through continual contact with the other languages and cultures added some new customs and modified the way

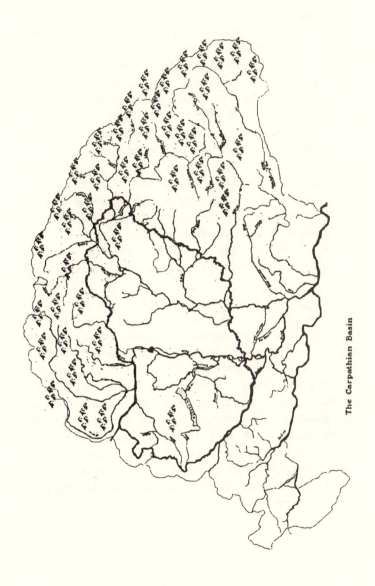

The Carpathian Basin

of life, indeed, but the dominance of its Hungarian character has never been threatened. As for the vying European religions, they are all represented in the buffer state of Hungary. While Catholicism dominated South-Western Europe and Protestantism the norther countries, they both found fertile soil in Hungary, along with the Greek Orthodox religion of the East. The endeavour of the Pan-Slav movement, whose champions were basically Czechs and Slovaks, was and still is apparent inside and outside the Carpathian Basin. Its close ties first with imperialistic Russia and then with the Soviet Union demonstrated expansionistic and domineering quality. While the fall of the Soviet Empire was only a question of time, the old Russian-Pan-Slav threat will not dissolve so easily. The Pan-Slavic movement, the present like its past, shows no sign or willingness to give up its desire to assimilate their non-Slav neighbours. The difficulty at present is that the Slovaks despise the Czechs, the Poles have been in perpetual conflict with the Russians and the Croatians disdain the Serbians. Everything is in a state of flux, attesting to the dynamics of history.

If we look at the map representing the situation before Trianon (1920), one sees that Hungary was surrounded by the Habsburg Empire with its Polish, Czech-Moravian, Austro-German, Southern-Slav elements, three parts Slav, two parts German. The non-Slav Hungarians constitute a wedge in this German_Slav sea, and an obstacle to the unification of the Slavs. Of the Pan-Slav movement and its purpose, Carl Marx, their prophet, writes thus: "Pan_Slavism is not merely a Slav expansionist ambition, but more so the striving for the destruction of a millennium of history. To realize this, half of Germany and all of Turkey must be erased from the map. After that the conquest of Europe may follow. Europe has two choices: the acceptance of the Pan-Slav designs or the subdual of Russia, the powder-magazine of the Slavik ambitions."[6]

CHAPTER 3

The Czech Conspiracy

In the history of nations, sixty-five years is nothing. Historians think in terms of centuries and millennia. Perspective is needed to evaluate things. One should not think of history as events recorded in the spirit of objectivity. In the age of monarchies, it was the kings' chroniclers who recorded the events. Flattery or national pride set the tone in many cases. Many a times, the distinction between legends and facts were obscured. Still, these old sources are useful in our age of literary criticism.

Focusing on the German and Czech publications written prior to the Treaties of Trianon, it should not be surprising that for political or national expediency misinformation, errors, omissions, biases and deliberate deceptions were very much the practice of the time. As far back as the tenth century, after the Magyars settled in the Carpathian Basin, German chroniclers of the Middle Age recorded that the outcome of the Battle of Augsburg (955) was a great and glorious for the Germans and a crushing defeat to the Magyars. The fact that the Hungarians did not suffer a "crushing defeat" was evident, because if they had, the Germans would have pursued the armies of the Magyar Ruler, Taksony (950-970). Instead, the Germans retreated and so did the Magyars. The German chroniclers failed to mention that the Czech units in the Hungarian army changed sides in mid battle, going over to the German side. Once the Hungarian commanders realized the treason, the Magyars retreated. Further omission by the German historians of the period was that after the battle, Otto I. German Emperor did not dare to invade Hungary, nor did his son, Otto II. or his grandson, Otto III. Thus, the first treason of the Czechs against the Hungarians was buried in historic obscurity.

Historical accounts often accuse the Hungarians as being no more than vassals of the German Empire. German emperors did, indeed, make attempts to bring this about, but the Magyars always resisted and they fought wars to preserve their independence. The Czech kings, on the other hand, were willing servants of the German emperors. To quote the Hungarian historian, Dezső Dümmerth:

> "As the German chronicler Thietmar writes, the Pope sent the crown and his blessing to Stephen, King of Hungary, on the urge of Otto the Emperor. The Emperor himself did not have the right to send a crown even at the height of his power. Apart from the Pope, the Byzantine Emperor alone had that right.... It occurred later, first in 1086, then again in 1158, that a German Emperor granted the royal title to a Czech prince. However, neither of these could be transmitted by inheritance. The latter was revoked when its bearer proved unworthy. The third case was a grant of Philip in 1198 which was confirmed by the Pope in 1203 after the confirmation of Otto IV. The Czech king was obviously a vassal of the German ruler.[7]"

And later, out of concern for self preservation and as a political necessity, the Czechs were always the most faithful attendants of the Habsburgs, and as no surprise, they felt wronged and neglected by the 1867 compromise between Austria and Hungary.

Present reassessment of European history, through credible witnesses, state documents, secret agreements, archival data collaborate the events which created and maintained the sixty-five year old Czechoslovakian Republic. In yesterday's Hungary, occupied by the Soviets, no one could write about these events, of course, except for their own locked drawers, in hope that future historians would find them and disclose the complete history of Northern Hungary.

As the first President of the Czechoslovak Republic, G.T. Masaryk, once said: "Without Benes, we should not have a republic."

One can say this of Masaryk as well. Without Masaryk and Benes, Czechoslovakia would not have been placed on the map of Europe. The Slovak politicians did not have in mind a union with the Czechs, in fact most wanted complete autonomy for their people. In 1939, thanks to Hitler, the Slovak dream did come to realization lasting only five years.

The politics of Masaryk and Benes before the first world war was aimed at uniting the anti-German forces. Since the Austro-Hungarian Monarchy was tied to Germany by treaties, they launched their propaganda campaign against the Monarchy. Urging the co-operation of the Central-European peoples, they proposed the reorganization of the region under Slav domination, guided by the people "most civilized and educated", that is to say, the Czechs. Their real purpose was the unification of all Slavs even if it meant dismemberment of Hungary. They believed, a confederation of Czechs, Slovaks, Serbians, Croatians and possibly Rumanians would be strong enough to withstand the pressure of Germany. It appears that Hungary was an obstacle to Slav unity, which Benes meant to overcome. The 'Czech Conspiracy' was formed, whose first act was to win the co-operation of the media in order to mesmerize the masses into believing that the dismemberment of Hungary was essential for the security of the region. Karel Kramar, a leading Czech political figure before the First World War, who was imprisoned by Austrian authorities for his Czech nationalistic views, after his release became a fierce adversary of Benes. He believed that Benes was using morally unacceptable means in his political manoeuvres.

The relationship between the Magyars and the Czechs was aggravated by the Slovak question. Masaryk and Benes worked for the annexation of Northern Hungary, where most of the Slovaks lived. The Hungarian government, on the other hand, defended the integrity of Hungary by trying to hold onto the few gains made in the Compromise of 1867. Vienna, although willing to experiment with the concept of an Austro-Czech Compromise, was persuaded by the Hungarian government not to commit itself to any agreement which may be detrimental to the integrity of Hungarian.

Part II

The Benes dream, as expounded in his pamphlet "Detruisez L'Autriche-Hongrie" served as a concrete program to the Czech Conspiracy. It read in part that:

> "The brutality of the Germans, Austrians and Hungarians comes from the same root... The Hungarians are the traditional allies of Germany, most faithful to them... They are of the same mind... The Hungarians are the pillars of the Central-European oppressors... They prevented the unification of the Serbians and Croatians, exploited Bosnia and Herzegovina... The Hungarians dare to claim access to the Aegean Sea..."

The above allegations were ill willed, ill founded and historically incorrect, however the western press received it ready-made. And when no opposition or objection was raised to Benes' pamphlet, Masaryk went further and asserted that, "the Hungarians were responsible for the outbreak of the First World War." The silence of politicians, diplomats, press-attachés or journalists to this blatant hate mongering was deafening. The Hungarian failure to cultivating foreign diplomatic and political allies and to listen to the ravings of the Czech separatists, cost Hungary dearly at the Treaty of Trianon.

Masaryk and the Czech Conspiracy knew the history of the Habsburg Monarchy very well, yet they were silent about the anti-Habsburg revolution of Kossuth's Hungary. They were silent about the century old German Czech alliances. They vehemently argued, that the Czech units had fought against the Hungarians in 1848, in order to defend the Slovaks. Documents from that period clearly indicate that Czech participation was motivated by political and economic needs to secure certain privileges from the Vienna camarilla in return for their loyalty. In 1918, the Czech separatists posed as the friends of Slovaks in Paris, London and Washington conferences. Skilfully the Conspiracy shifted its views as political expediency dictated! They accredited the German Chancellor, Bismarck, as saying that he did not annex Austria, because Austria was the beach-head against the expansion of the East. Bismark never said that. Benes invented it. As for Masaryk, he often read the pages of the Frantisek Palacky's historical journal and readily adopted the writer's accusations that, "the Hungarians separated the Czechs and Slovaks from the Slavs of the South."

The Czech Conspiracy seized upon the idea. A corridor must be created between Czechoslovakia and Yugoslavia! They advocated that, the Slav unification must proceed for the good of Europe, even if it means dismembering Hungary. They further argued that this shall secure eternal peace. Masaryk and his companions could not forgive the presence of Hungarians, because the presence of Hungary was an obstacle to the formation of a Slav Empire in Central Europe.

Benes was treacherous in his efforts to win the western politicians. When he saw that his cause was far from bringing general support, he changed his method. He posed as the champion of democracy, humanism and world peace. In that period his articles published in the "friendly" papers spoke not of the future Czecho-Slovak republic but of the excellence of his people, the brave Czechs, who had struggled against the German Giant for centuries. He did not elaborate on the Czech voluntary adoption of German culture and language. During the last century and a half, while the Czech language was mainly used in the country, the large Czech cities like Prague carried German store signs and the general population conversed in their official language, which was German. The 1348 German founded University of Prague, did not provide courses in Czech until 1882. When Masaryk was offered a professorship at the university he hesitated to accept, because he did not speak Czech well.

The Benes rhetoric, fuelled by the support of the Czech Conspiracy, continued: "The Czech nation is the hero of democracy and humanism!" Benes counting on the historical ignorance of the masses, appealed to the whole western world asking it to help shake off their shackles. "God created the Czechs to be the pillars of democracy and the guardians of peace over the barbarian German, Hungarian, Mongol and Tartar tribes." In order to follow this mission, he argued,

Part II

"the Czechs must be liberated from the oppression of the Austro-Hungarian Monarchy. The Czechs must be united with the Slovaks and Yugoslavs! Think of the interest of Europe, your own interest!"

CHAPTER 4

Masaryk and Benes

Masaryk and Benes met in the initial days of the First World War. Their political views were initially different. Masaryk, the university professor, editor of "Cas" (Time) was a rationalist. Benes, teacher in a commercial school, and a regular contributor to the Social-Democratic party publication "Pravo Lidu" (The Right of the People) and to the "Volna Myslenka" (Free Thought), was a radical. However, both of them were students of Western Democracy and both mistrusted absolutism, Prussian militarism, feudalism and the aristocracy. Masaryk took note of Benes' journalistic work, and soon Benes found himself as Masaryk's confidant. Together they read the latest issues of the London "Morning Post" and "Times", sent to Masaryk by Seaton Watson (Scotus Viator), English journalist and ardent supporter of the Pan-Slav movement. Expanding their circle of supporters, Masaryk and Benes with loyal followers formed the Czech Conspiracy.

At the beginning of the world war, Masaryk sent Benes to France and he himself went to London, England. They maintained a close contact, informing each other of their respective difficulties or success. Benes, taking note of Western ignorance about Central European history, effectively built his diplomacy on their naivete. The organization of his compatriots was harder. Due to the centuries old connections with Austria, the mentality of the ordinary Czech citizen, and especially that of the aristocracy, was far less nationalistic than the one advocated by the Masaryk-Benes clique. The political adversary of Benes, Karel Kramar, saw the "liberation" of the Czechs in the support of the Russian Tzars. As a result, Benes did not enjoy Czech popularity during the war. He was hardly known by the Czech people when, in 1918, he became Foreign Minister. His political adversaries seized every opportunity to discredit him. He was a poor man when he arrived in Paris and lived in a rented room. Without the support of his well-to-do friends he could not have started his propaganda campaign. One of his principal supporters was Milan Stefanik, a

Slovak serving as a colonel in charge of an air wing in the French army. Benes let him into the secret plan conceived by Masaryk and himself, inviting Stefanik to be one of the founding fathers of the future Czechoslovak state. Stefanik, a nationalist himself, liked the idea. Benes passed on the good news to Masaryk, recommending the colonel for the post of Minister of War. Stefanik, general by that time, went to Italy to recruit among the Czech and Slovak prisoners of war and set up a Czech-Slovak legion. His mission was not to last long. In 1919 he became a victim of an airplane crash at Pozsony. He took the secrets regarding the future autonomous Slovakia into his grave. Later the Slovak National Council urged an investigation of the air crash, in vain. The Czech Conspiracy, or Benes himself, prevented the investigation.

General Stefanik knew about the agreement between Masaryk and the American Slovaks made in Pittsburg in the June of 1918, and also about the millions of dollars raised among the Slovak emigrants for the purposes of the Czech propaganda. The political adversaries of Benes accused him of embezzlement. The question of his suddenly acquired wealth was raised in the Prague Parliament by Jan Sramek, the leader of the People's Party. Vlastimil Tusar Prime Minister replied: "Monseigneur, revolutions are not made under the rules of accounting!" Why, was there a Czech revolution? The questioning and the criticism continued. Jiri Stribny, a National-Socialist MP, General Rudolf Gajda, the organizer of the Siberian-Czech legion, and Karel Pergler, once a colleague of Masaryk, later ambassador in Tokyo and Washington, joined forces against Benes. Benes had to give an account before the parliament. Masaryk eventually admitted that, in 1922, as President of the newborn Republic he received ten million crowns from the Czech people as an expression of their gratitude. Of this, he gave two million crowns to Benes. However, the fate of the millions of dollars donated by the American Slovaks is still undisclosed. People believed that they owed their rise to the Western World. Few were aware of the manipulation of dark forces behind the friendly tone of the foreign press. They did not know of the sordid intrigues of Benes and his fellow conspirators.

Benes was Foreign Minister of Czechoslovakia for seventeen years, until 1935. He knew very well that his state acquired what it did with the help of the Western Allies and these acquisitions could be kept only through the continual support of these Allies. Therefore he frequently visited his western friends. Lacking oratory and statesman qualities, Benes was a rather colourless, dry and cold individual. The prototype of a clerk, he felt best at his desk. Publicly he insisted on democratic principles, nevertheless, when he was empowered to make political decisions, he became a sort of dictator, jealously guarding his power. His talents, diligence and his undaunted chauvinism had raised him from the simple surroundings of his birth to the "Hradzsin" of Prague. He was convinced that he and no one else could worthily represent his country.

After the outbreak of the first world war, both Masaryk and Benes believed that the Austro-Hungarian Monarchy would be on the losing side and its collapse was inevitable. As early as the summer of 1914, Masaryk went to Holland "to prepare the soil". Thanks to his connections with Seaton Watson, Benes' anti-Hungarian articles regularly appeared in the London Morning Post and the Times. When Masaryk returned to Prague, Benes was already there, organizing the Czech Conspiracy. Joining forces, the two built cells in Austria, Germany and Switzerland. They received the English papers sent by Watson through Germany and Switzerland. In December 1914, Masaryk went to Rome. Before his departure he had given instructions and left a manifesto for distribution in case the Russian troops should occupy Prague. In Rome he met Stefanik, the organizer of the Czech legion in Italy. He arranged for the printing of leaflets that were sent to the Russian front, with the help of the British Headquarters, and later scattered over the Slovak and Czech regiments. The leaflet contained the Slav national song "Hej Slovane" (Now then Slovak). The war prisoners singing this song were assembled in separate camps. Whole Czech regiments surrendered. It turned out that the Czechs were fighting in the common army of the Austrians and Hungarians, while the Slovaks mostly in the Hungarian regiments.

When Masaryk moved to Geneva, that city became the headquarters for the Czech Conspiracy. Its spies operated undisturbed in neutral Switzerland. Under various names and forged passports Benes himself went to Geneva several times, for strategic consultations with Masaryk. he Austrian government bureaus abounded in Czech employees who willingly co-operated. To give an example, the Austrian Minister of the Interior, Baron Karl Heinold, had a Czech servant, Julius Kovanda, who copied a number of confidential letters and documents from the desk of his employer and passed them on to Jozef Machar, an officer of the Czech General Staff, and they ended up in the hands of Masaryk. The Conspiracy had its secret agents everywhere, even in places like the Sokol Sport Club. he Austrian Police force could not unmask the organization for a long time, for the agents were warned in advance of any house searches planned.

On the 20th of May, 1915, after a lengthy investigation, Kramar and several members of the Sokol Sport Club were arrested. They found pamphlets, english and french papers in Kramar's home. Soon after Benes learned about the Kramar arrest, he fled across the frontier of Germany and later, with the help of a forged passport, he arrived in Geneva. From there Benes was sent to Paris and in the meantime, Lev Sychrava was placed in charge of the Geneva headquarters. Masaryk himself moved to London, where he became the professor of Slav studies in the King's College, thanks to his connections. Soon, other cells in Washington, Petrograd and Rome were cultivated.

The Czech propaganda, under the direction of Benes, did all in its power to enhance the image of the Czechs and present the Hungarians as uncivilized. Initially, this propaganda campaign encountered difficulties. Many Western politicians did not know about the Czechs any more than they did about the Hungarians. In the late eighteen hundreds, American and British historians wrote favourably about the democratic endeavour of Kossuth, approving his idea of a Danubian Confederation and admiring his role in Hungary's fight for freedom in 1848. Kossuth was widely seen as the champion of freedom and democracy. Masaryk and Benes went to all lengths to destroy this nimbus of Kossuth. They published numerous articles in which the Hungarians were called anti-democratic, oppressors of minorities, vassals of the tyrants of Austria. However, the Czech Conspiracy incessantly ran against sympathy towards the Hungarians especially in Western publications.

Statesmen, journalist and historians publicly expressed the need for a strong and well established state to occupy the centre of Europe. For example: Frantisek Palacky, the well known Czech historian wrote about Austria in 1848 "... Indeed, if the Austrian Monarchy did not exist, it would be necessary to create it in the interest of Europe." As well, in the book by Prince Otto and entitled "Gedanken und Erinnerungen", Bismark asks the question "What could be placed in the area of the Austrian state between Tirol and Bukovina? New formations in this area would breed incessant revolutions." In 1874 Bismark proclaimed, "In Eastern Europe the creation of little states is unthinkable. Only states of long history can thrive there." Even Woodrow Wilson, the President of the United States made the following remark before Congress in 1917, "It is not our intention to weaken or transform the Austro-Hungarian Monarchy. Nor do we want to interfere in their economic system or politics. It is in our interest that those peoples should retain their power and independence." And then, Lloyd George, British Prime Minister stated on January 5th, 1918, "The dissolution of the Austro-Hungarian Monarchy is not among our objectives."[8]

Masaryk himself acknowledges in his writing "Sventove Revoluce", that in America, as well as elsewhere, it had been very hard to spread the belief that the breakup of the Austro-Hungarian Monarchy was desirable. For Austria was widely considered the counterpoise of Germany, a protective force against Balkanization. The sympathy for Austria, which was prevalent until 1918 in Western government circles, was manifested in President Wilson's statements.

The Masaryk disclosure was made in order to emphasize the value of his efforts by which he eventually succeeded in creating a smoke screen. He and his agents were successful in confusing some of the leading Western statesman. So much so that in September of 1918, less than nine months after his pro Austria-Hungary statement made before Congress, President Wilson told Károly IV, the King of Hungary, that he had changed his opinion and that he could no longer support a self-governing Monarchy. He added that the price of peace would be the autonomy of the ethnic groups within the area, that is, the dissolution of the Monarchy.

How did Masaryk and Benes manage this radical change of attitude? References to Masaryk's letter written to the son of Oxenstierna, a Swedish statesman, provides some enlightenment. Masaryk writes, "Can't you see, my dear son, how little wisdom is put in the government of this world?" But more so in his book entitled "Svetove Revoluce", Masaryk clearly outlines his Machiavellian modus operandi. He attributes great importance to his connections. He was not choosy. Apart from the Czech Conspiracy and other secret organizations, a number of bribed clerks and civil servants, journalist obliged to him, valets, fanatics of the cause, constituted the core of these connections. Through these connections Masaryk and his companions were extremely well informed of events behind the scenes, in the private affairs of persons of importance. They knew who's voices were weighty. They knew the weaknesses of these influential men and exploited them. They knew of secret agreements between nations as well. "The worth of a man is the sum of his talents minus his vanity", said Bismark once. Masaryk knew this and constantly used the wisdom of psychology. He confessed in his reminiscences, that he won over President Wilson through sheer flattery. He obtained the service of others by gifts and promises. The essence of their strategy was to win the leaders and men of high rank. They never wasted time on subordinates, only used them. The means and methods were carefully selected and coordinated. Whenever he suggested to Wilson something he was not prepared to accept, within a few days some article would appear in the papers to justify Masaryk's views. At last Wilson was obliged to see in Masaryk a man of foresight who should be heeded. And last, but not least, Masaryk's weapons included intrigues woven in a masterly manner, distorted in masterly deception.

CHAPTER 5

Machiavellism

In the records of the peace-negotiations between 1918 and 1920, the sense of bad conscience and doubt is manifest. Some of the negotiators felt, others knew, that serious troubles would inevitably arise, if the centuries old unity of the Monarchy should be replaced by the pall-mall proposed by Masaryk and Benes. But at the time, expression was not given to the negotiators' anxiety, except in a few timid objections. They seemed to be under a spell. As if a mysterious power had muffled the voice of their conscience.

Wilson had two objections against the creation of Czechoslovakia. One was that the Czechs had not proven their capability of forming a state. The other had to do with numbers. He believed that a people numbering six and a half million should not be dominant over minorities with a combined population approaching their own. Wilson's first concern was dispelled by the legend of the Siberian Czech legions. The American President believed the myth invented by Masaryk and saw it as a proof of the maturity of the Czechs as a nation. To dissolve the President's second concern, Masaryk invented the fiction of the Czechoslovak people. When this odd phrase did not have the desired effect, Masaryk quickly signed an agreement with the Slovaks living in the United States. The Pittsburg agreement, signed in June 30, 1918, was then presented to Wilson as proof of a Czech-Slovak federative treaty. In this 'treaty', which was signed without sanction from any legal state, Masaryk promised full autonomy to the Slovak people and contained a guarantee, that their national aspirations would not be interfered with. The Masaryk promise was never fulfilled. Having seen the treaty, Wilson acknowledged a provisional Czechoslovak state. Three years later Masaryk declared; "There is no Slovak nation. It is the invention of the Hungarians"[9]. As for the Pittsburg agreement, he stated: "We signed the agreement in order to soothe a small Slovak group which had dreams of independence".

Part II

During the peace negotiations several delegates felt anxiety about the fate of the populous minorities which would fall within the frontiers of Czechoslovakia proposed by Andre Tardieu, a French delegate Benes hastened to calm the dissenting elements. In a memorandum, dated 20 May, 1919, he assured all those preparing the peace treaty that Czechoslovakia would become a sort of Switzerland where the various nationalities would live in peace and freedom. And four months later, on 10 september, 1919, Benes signed the treaty of Saint Germain-en-Lay, in which the Czechoslovak government pledged full respect for the rights of the minorities.

The Allies were not against the Austro-Hungarian Monarchy. They saw it as a natural and political barrier to German expansion. In British political circles the plan to destroy the Monarchy was considered madness. They wanted a re-organized Habsburg Monarchy. In December 1917, Lloyd George, The Prime Minister of England, commissioned General J. Christian Smuts to talk with Albert Mensdorff-Ponilly, the former London ambassador of the Monarchy. General Smuts disclosed the proposal of his government. According to this plan Galicia would be annexed to Poland and this enlarged Poland would form a union with the future Monarchy. The Serbian State would consist of Serbia, Herzegovina and Montenegro. Bukovina would be annexed to Rumania. The Rumanians living in Transylvania had the impression that England did not insist on the annexation of Transylvania to Rumania.

Benes learned about Britain's plan through the Czech Conspiracy operating in Switzerland. He thought it was catastrophic and worked day and night on a memorandum to the Allied Powers in an attempt to show the absurdity of the federalization of Austria. While in his early years at the Dijon University, Benes once entertained the idea of federation, however, not fitting his present plans, he vehemently opposed it. Masaryk, too, saw a great menace to their dreams in the British plan. He did not want autonomy for his people within a federalized monarchy. Characteristic of their thinking, they would have approved a federation of Russia and Poland but favoured independence for the Southern Slavs. To reconcile the Italians, because the Yugoslav ambitions were against the interests of Italy, Masaryk promised them the help of the Czech legion, which were formed in Rome.

Did Masaryk and Benes have any moral or worthwhile conception for the reorganization and future of Central Europe? As more documents and records come to light, the clearer it becomes that both Masaryk and Benes were dazed by a sort of muddled Jacobinistic nationalism and personal ambitions.

CHAPTER 6

The Road to Trianon

Published Western accounts of, and comments on, the dictated Peace Treaty of Trianon would fill a library. And although, there is mention of Hungary's political stand in the aftermath of the great confrontation, two major questions have yet to be answered by the West. One, what was the role of the Czech propaganda and the secret agreements made by the Czech Conspiracy during the First World War? The other, what effect did the months long takeover by the Communist in Hungary have on Allied policies, and why in the end did it resulted in such a harsh and unfair peace treaty?

The chronological order of events, which lead from a localized confrontation to a major world event was set off by a successful assassination plot, which found as its target, Ferdinand, the heir apparent to the Monarchy and his wife, on June 28, 1914. Leopold Berchtold, the Foreign Minister of the Monarchy informed Count István Tisza, the Prime Minister of Hungary, that he considered the murder at Sarajevo as Serbia's Declaration of War. The Monarchy was irresistibly drifting towards a major world war. On July 7, 1914, Berchtold disclosed to the Vienna Camarilla his views in support of sending an ultimatum to Serbia. István Tisza advised the council to first send a memorandum, indicating the Emperor's demands, but phrased in a more friendly tone. The memorandum was then delivered, on July 19, to the Serbian government by Baron Giesel. As Tisza suggested, it included an assurance from the Monarchy that it had no intention of annexing Serbia if the Monarchy's demands were met. Serbia rejected the memorandum. Immediately, Austro-Hungary mobilized its forces. In his note to the Emperor, Tisza strongly opposed the idea of a war. However, he felt it was not prudent to publish the contents of his note. As a result, Masaryk seising the right moment for effect, charged that the Hungarian Prime Minister was responsible for the outbreak of the war. It was only after the release of the documents in the Vienna Kriegs archives that it became apparent that Masaryk's charge was groundless.

On the advice of Berchtold and the Chief of Staff, Conrad von Hötzendorf, Emperor Franz Josef I. declared war on Serbia. The flame of war quickly spread all over Europe. By August of 1914, Germany mobilized against Russia and France. Next, the German army invaded Belgium, which brought about the intervention of England. The Russians mobilized and sent their army to the frontier of the Austro-Hungarian Monarchy. Inevitably, the Monarchy expanded its struggle against Russia.

In the meanwhile, the Czech Conspiracy, seeing their opportunity, dispatched Jiri Klecanda, a Czech politician, to Petrograd. His clandestine task was to offer "the crown of St. Vaclar" to the Romanovs. In response to this offer, the Czar of Russia instructed Archduke Nikolaj Nikolajevics, the Commander-in-Chief of the Russian Army, to grant complete amnesty to all Czechs who surrender. By November, Czech prisoners of war were organized into combat units, under the direction of the Russian Ministry of War. About the same time, Masaryk dispatched his first proposal on the dismemberment of the Monarchy to his followers. While the Austro-Hungarian and Hungarian divisions were engaged in a desperate fight against the superior forces of Russia, whole Czech regiments surrendered to the enemy. As a result of the Czech desertions, by October of 1914, the Hungarian Territorial Army was over powered and broken.

The following February, Masaryk departed Rome and, using a forged passport, arrived in Geneva to build useful connections between the emigres and the Conspiracy. In March of 1915, he launched a Paris periodical, "La Nation Tcheque" (The Czech Nation). The first issue contained Masaryk's dream map of Czechoslovakia with its borders reaching down to the Danube. Hastily, he leaves the periodical to the care of Benes and moves on to London, England. From London, in a political pamphlet, "Independent Bohemia", he advocated for the need of a federative Czecho-slovak state. During his London stay, Seaton Watson introduced him to Sir George Russel Clark, the head of the British Foreign Office. Masaryk, needing to make an ally of Clark, explained to him the objectives of the Czech exiles. Not wanting to loose the momentum, he next presented a memorandum to the Secretary of Foreign Affairs, Sir Edward Grey, in which he offered the Czech throne to the Grand Duke of the Romanovs. Failing that, he offered the throne to any member of the Karageorgevich dynasty, in return for the formation of a Southern Slav State. By way of precaution, or else to forestall any protest, Masaryk refrained from suggesting that the Slovak people should be placed under Czech domination. With the fall of the Przemysl Fortress on March 22, 1915, the Russian victory in Galicia is inevitable, and with it the hopes of the Czech Conspirators heightened. Masaryk in London, Benes in Paris, Stefanik in Rome and Gajda in Moscow were weaving the threads of diplomacy. Closely coordinated, the foursome jointly issued a "Declaration" in May of 1915, and sent it to the governments of the Allies.

Masaryk's well-organized propaganda network worked. It won the sympathy of influential members in Western governments and the support of numerous English and French journalists. However, two difficulties arose. The propaganda campaign failed to convince the majority of the Slovaks that the creation of a Republic was such a good idea. The Slovaks were well aware that they depended on the crops of the Great Hungarian Plain. From the counties of Lipto and Árva, some ten thousand harvesters travelled to the Plain every summer to earn money, essential to support their families. At the end of the harvest, long freight trains rolled toward Northern Hungary loaded with provisions.[10] Scores of carriages and carts were waiting at their destinations for the life-sustaining crates and cases. It was obvious that the ordinary Slovak worker was not enthusiastic about the idea of a Republic. And while the Slovak populous was not inclined towards separating from Hungary, their intellectuals were even less receptive to a the idea of a political betrothal to the Czechs. The Pan-Slavists were but a fraction of the Slovak people. They would have been satisfied with a certain degree of autonomy and the preservation of their language and cultural traditions.

The other difficulty that Masaryk and his friends encountered was monetary in nature. During the world war, it was not easy to get financial support. The potential backers felt the inflation. The support of the Russians came to a stop. And the propaganda network was very costly. The practical Czechs realized, that the help of their emigrated compatriots was needed. There was a price of course. On the October 15, 1915, Czech Conspiracy made an agreement with the Slovaks at Pittsburg. According to this agreement the Slovak territory in Northern Hungary would enjoy self-government, with a Parliament of its own. It was also understood that the use of the Slovak language would be guaranteed and respected. With the signing of the Pittsburg Accord the donations began to flow in.

A month later, on November 14, the "Czech Committee Abroad" was formed. It published its first manifesto on the cause of the Czechoslovak independence. The Czech associations in foreign lands joined the Paris committee. In January, 1916, Benes produced his pamphlet "Detruisez l'Autriche-Hongrie", in which he demanded the liberation of the Slav population from the Monarchy and the unification of the Southern Slavs. On page 62 of the pamphlet, he remarked, that "the map of the new Czechoslovakia cannot be shown, because of French censorship". On the advice from French politicians, in February of 1916, the Committee changed its name to "Conseil National des Pays Tcheques" (The Czech National Council). Later the name was amended to include the slovak representation. Masaryk became Committee President, Benes was named Secretary-General, and Stefanik was to represent the Slovak elements. From conception, the Committee operated as the Provisional Czechoslovak Government in exile. To support its cause, Seaton Watson was called upon to popularize the idea of an enlarged Czechoslovakian State, which he did in his pamphlet entitle, "German, Slav and Hungarian". Masaryk, to show a united front, called on all Czech and Slovak organizations operating in foreign countries to join his committee. In response, the Czechs living in Russia signed the Kiev Manifesto, in December of 1916, subordinating themselves to the wishes of the National Council in Paris. According to the Kiev joint council records, in 1916, the Czech and Slovak emigrants in Russia operated 113 political, 123 prisoner of war and 95 military associations.

CHAPTER 7

The Expropriation of
Northern Hungary

The Emperor-King, Franz Joseph I. died on November 21, 1916. His nephew, the Habsburg-Lotharing Carl succeeded him to the throne as Emperor Carl I. and Károly IV. King of Hungary. Immediately after his coronation, the new Emperor set out to achieve peace. He asked his brother-in-law, Sixtus, Prince of Parma, to approach the French Foreign Ministry in order to prepare a possible separate peace for Austria and Hungary. Advocating reconciliation among the various nationalities, Carl I. granted amnesty to Karel Kramar, who was sentenced to death. Sixtus met with Raymond Poincare, the President of the French Republic on March 8, 1917. Poincare showed willingness to forward a formal peace-proposal of the Monarchy to the English and Russian rulers. The peace initiative failed, because of the objections raised by the Italian Government.

Objecting to the separate peace proposals, István Tisza, the Prime Minister of Hungary, tenders his resignation in March of 1917 and a period of short-lived governments begins. Móric Eszterházy's government was quickly followed by that of Sándor Wekerle. Wekerle, with the approval of the Monarch, made an effort to redefine the relationship of Austria and Hungary. Unfortunately, the pressure of events toppled the government and the power passed to the "National Council". The Monarchy, having taken the unfortunate advice of the left-wing radicals, appointed Count Mihály Károlyi as the new Prime Minister and head of the National Council. Shortly after assuming his office, Károlyi petitioned the Monarch to release him from his oath. It was granted. Now the way was paved for the revolt of the uninhibited left-wing radicals and socialists. Next, the Monarchy freed the military from their oath of allegiance.

Hungary was left to drift in the sea of conflict, like a boat, floundering without a rudder, facing the leading edge of a second storm. The chronical enumeration of events reflected the drama of 1918:

October 9 - the Czech members of parliament left the Vienna "Reichsrat";

October 14 - Benes informed the Allies of the establishment of a provisional Czechoslovak government;

October 15 - France acknowledged the provisional government;

October 18 - Wilson, the President of the United States rejected the peace proposal of the Monarchy, which would have guaranteed autonomy for the Czechs, Slovaks and Southern Slavs. Instead, Wilson acknowledged the Czechoslovak government;

October 28 - The Czech National Council in Prague and the leaders of the four Czech parties declared the formation of the Czechoslovak Republic;

October 30 - The Slovak National Council at Turocszentmárton announced the separation of Slovensko from Hungary;

November 6 - Czech legions crossed the Moravian-Hungarian frontier at Hodonin;

November 8 - The victorious Allies summoned Károlyi to Belgrade for armistice talks.

What was the general opinion of Hungary in allied circles? It was manifested in the words of Franchet d'Esperey, the head of the armistice committee: "Vous etéz déja tombé si ba?" (How have you sunk so low?)

The Belgrade Armistice directed Serbia to occupy the Hungarian counties of Bánát, Bácska, Muraköz and southern part of

Vas, Zala, Somogy and Baranya, including the cities of Pécs and Baja. In Belgrade, the occupation of Northern Hungary was not decided, the subject did not even come up. In the North and North-East, the historical frontier remained the line of demarcation. The unauthorised invasion of the Czech regiments was an arbitrary action. The Károlyi government looked on without moving a finger, even forbade the Hungarian military forces to resist.

Rutter Owen wrote in his book, "Regent of Hungary" (London, 1939): "Hungary would not have fallen under Bolshevik domination, had the Allies prevented the succession states from overrunning the territories, which they expected to get as the result of the peace-negotiations in progress."[11] This catastrophe must be attributed to the extraordinary influence of the Czech politicians in Paris. "These politicians obtained the Allies' approval for the occupation of predominantly Hungarian areas, when the relating peace-treaty had not been signed, nay, its text had not even been published."[12] Since the provisional Czechoslovak government was still waiting for the final decision of the Allies on the fate of Northern Hungary, it sent a commissioner, Emil Stodola, to Budapest on November 12, instructing him to confer with the Károlyi government about the withdrawal of the troops on both sides. The Czech government proposed the occupation of Northern Hungary by the Allied forces until the peace-treaty was to take effect. The talks proceeded smoothly until the Czechoslovak Revolutionary National Assembly in Prague went into action. The assembly, which was set up through a coalition of five parties: the Czech Agrarian Party of Svehla, the Czech National-Socialist Party of Klofac, the Czech National Democratic Party of Kramar, the Catholic People's Party of Sramek and the Social-Democrats, numbered 212 representatives. It was significant that, where an equal Czech and Slovak parliamentary representation was promised by Masaryk, out of the 212 delegate positions only 44 were given to the Slovaks.

The Provisional Czechoslovak National Assembly, next declared the dethronement of the Habsburgs, and proclaimed the new Czechoslovak Republic. Tomas G. Masaryk became the new republics' president, with Karel Kramar as Prime Minister, Eduárd Benes as Foreign Minister, Alois Rasin as Minister of Finance and Milan Rastislav Stefanik as Minister of War. Kramar dispatched a note to Károlyi, in which he called the Czech military operations in Northern Hungary justified and internationally supported. The same day, Czech legions began the occupation of the cities of Trencsén and Nagyszombat. Instead of reacting to the Czechoslovak insurgence, Hungary's National Council, on November 16, 1918, proclaimed the new state of the Hungarian People's Republic.[13]

The sombre Hungarian politicians and citizens, who had heard of the manifestations of the Bolshevik terror in Russia, had reason to hope that the Allies would check the aggressions of Hungary's neighbours. No Allied intervention was forth coming. Memoirs written between the two world wars revealed that the peace-negotiators were greatly influenced by two facts: they saw Hungary apparently drifting toward a system based on the Bolshevik pattern, whereas in the surrounding countries, especially in Czechoslovakia, western type democracy was loudly advocated.

In Hungary, the atrocities of the Bolshevik terror filled the whole population with horror. To prove it, the new Bolshevites like Tibor Samuely and Béla Kun, boasted that the "strongest weapon of our government is terror". To add to the suffering, a demoralized citizenry was further humiliated by Béla Linder, the Minister of War in the Károlyi government[14], who greeted the soldiers returning from the front by declaring that, "I do not want to see any more soldiers!"

This baleful slump was witnessed by Allied observers, like Colonel Alexander Fitzgerald, who sent a detailed report on the low state of Hungary's national moral to Sir Thomas Cunningham, an English commissioner in Vienna. General Bandholtz of the United States, who had prevented the Rumanians from pillaging the Royal Hungarian Palace and the Hungarian National Museum, described the events in Hungary in his memoirs "An undiplomatic Diary", with the authenticity of an eyewitness.

Part II

The Allies, On December 4, 1918, recognized the state of Czechs and authorized the Czech Army to occupy Northern Hungary, in order to exercise control over that territory until the conclusion of the peace treaty. What this administrative supervision meant, was nothing short of legalized plundering, robbery, removal of appliances from factories, seizing farm implements and furnishings of state and private citizens. The Czechs themselves did not expect that Kassa, Pozsony, Komárom and the Csallóköz would become theirs. Wyx, the French Lieutenant Colonel in charge of the Allied mission at Budapest, demanded the withdrawal of the Hungarian troops from those areas.

The dawn of 1919 brought further decimation to the territorial integrity of Hungary. On January 9, Brejcha, the Czech administrator of Ruthenia, and Hennoque, the French General in charge, signed a preliminary agreement with regard to the occupation of Ruthenia. According to clause 4. of the agreement, the elections of the Ruthenian "Szojun" (National Assembly) would be held within 90 days after the parliamentary elections in Czechoslovakia. The agreed upon Ruthenian election was never honoured.

The new Hungarian Republic's National Council, on January 11, proclaimed Károlyi as President. By January 19, the peace negotiations begun, with the participation of the Czech delegates (Masaryk, Benes, Kramar and Stefauik). Two months later, on March 21, the Hungarian Workers' Council announced the dictatorship of the proletariate, modelled on a Soviet republic. Károlyi was put aside and Hungary irresistibly sank toward communist anarchy. The international position of Hungary became precarious. The delegates of the Károlyi government were signatures at the issue of the Belgrade Conventions. But, the effect of the October revolution in Russia was felt more and more in Eastern Europe. Meanwhile, the Allies followed these developments with growing anxiety. In vain did Károlyi advocate "Wilsonian political principles", as far as the Allies were concern, it is too late. They did not trust Károlyi. The Hungarian extreme left regarded his idea as "bourgeois deviation". And when Károlyi attempted to advocate his Wilsonistic approach, no one listened. The extreme left agitated the proletariate for Leninism rather than Wilsonism. Non the less, Károlyi clung to Wilson's ideas, because he hoped that the peace conference would thus be more understanding to Hungarian concerns. Allied reports, on the other hand, revealed strong concerns, that Hungary's internal affairs were in the hands of agitators, who were Moscow trained.

In May, 1919, the Czech troops marched into Miskolc. The panic-stricken provisional government of Hungary offered peace to the Czechs and concessions to the Rumanians, who had also advanced as far as the Tisza river, with the reservation that the succession states will not meddle in the internal affairs of Hungary. The offer was refused by the Czechs and the Rumanians. They hoped for more. By now Red, the Hungarian Army engaged in several successful counterattacks and soon reached Bártfa at the country's historical frontier. The Hungarian military success was due to patriotic zeal. But on July 8, in response to France's ultimatum, the Hungarian Army was forced to withdraw from Northern Hungary.

George Clemenceau, the French Prime Minister distrusted and disliked the Germans and the Austro-Hungarian Monarchy. The Czernin - Clemencean affair preceded and influenced his ultimatum. The affair started at the beginning of 1918, about the time when the machinations of the Czechs ran into unexpected obstacles. The ominous events in Russia filled the Allies with anxiety. The preservation of the Austro-Hungarian Monarchy seemed desirable, not so much against the eastward expansion of Germany, as against the westward reaching of Russia. On January 5, 1919, George Lloyd, the English Prime minister declared that the dissolution of Austro-Hungary was not the objective of the English government. This statement was the cause of great worry among the Czechs because Clemencean shared Lloyd's view. However, United States President, Wilson, refused to accept anything short of full autonomy for the minorities within the Monarchy. Czernin, the Foreign Minister of the Monarchy, on January 8, formally accepted Wilson's 14 point plan. But there was an political altercation. For Czernin, on April 2, allegedly was quoted to say in a speech, that the French Prime Minister's alleged peace initiative failed, because France had no intention in relinquishing Alsace-Lorraine to Germany. This alleged accusation enraged Clemencean to the point where he publicly called Czernin a liar. And although it was a fact, that Germany wanted to regain possession of Alsace-Lorraine and France did not want to give it up, it is still not clear whether Czernin did indeed make the remark in an official capacity or just in a private conversation, or whether he even made such a remark at all. But when the peace-seeking efforts of the Austro-Hungarian Monarch leaked out through indiscretion, the worried Benes consulted Clemencean for advise and support is known. The Czernin-Clemencean affair did a great deal of harm to the prospects of peace.

Benes welcomed the Czernin-Clemenceau affair. "Inter duos litigantes terius gaudet" (Between the two combatants, the third will be glad). Benes was glad, for his great concern of Allied opposition to his plans just disappeared. When he met with Clemenceau at Quay d'Orsau, his deep dislike for the Germans and the Monarchy found resonance with the Frenchman. They decided that the legions set up by the Czech National Council in Paris would join the hostilities in order to create a legal ground for the formation of a provisional government. France became the principal supporter of Czech ambitions. Benes shrewdly fuelled Clemencean's feelings. "The Austro-Hungarian Monarchy is the vanguard of German imperialism", he said, "and the Hungarians are tools of German expansion towards the East". "Let them perish together with the Germans!", thundered Clemencean. And Benes' instigation continued. "The Hungarians are worse than the Germans", he said, "brutality originates from the Hungarians". So argued Benes. Clemencean completely accepted and sympathized with Benes' views. It was no wonder, that Hungary, a practically unknown and internationally isolated country, lost more than any other, even more than Germany, in the ensuing peace negotiations.[15]

During Versailles conferences, while the Allies readily accepted the establishment of the Polish state, in order to keep the Slav separatist movements in check and the United States Government showed understanding and gave importance to the findings of the Rome Congress, yet no final decision was made at the time. In the mean while, Benes went to great length to assure Pichon, the French Minister of foreign affairs, that the region of Northern Hungary, (he does not dare to call it Slovakia at the point), would attach itself to the Czech state, thus forming the new state "Czechoslovakia". Working against Benes, Lord Cecil Robert and James Balfour, Ministers of the English Cabinet, were not prepared to recognize the Czech National Council in Paris as the future government of Czechoslovakia, because of the uncertainty that the new order would be accepted by the local population. During the peace negotiations Benes repeatedly encountered British and American objections. Anticipated those objections, he always asked for more than he wanted to acquire. As an example: he demanded the highlands in the northern part of Eastern Hungary, including the city of Miskolc, and a corridor across Western Hungary to Yugoslavia.[16] When he presented his demands, Nicholson, a spokesman for the British Foreign Office, declared: "Je vous en prie, n'en parlez pas. C'est une betise!" If you please, do not speak so! This is nonsense."[17] This was not the only nonsense uttered by Benes. Unfortunately, the uninformed and superficial negotiators were more impressed by the fabrications of Benes than by the thoroughly substantiated facts enumerated by the Hungarian delegate, Count Apponyi.

Fabrications by members of the Provisional Czech Government deceived not only the Allies but also the Slovaks and the Ruthenians. Zsatkovich, the leader of the Ruthenians was misled by Benes, who claimed the drawing of Ruthenia's boundaries would only be tentative. When András Hlinka, the leader of the Slovak People's Party, arrived in Paris in order to make sure that the Pittsburg agreement between the Slovaks and the Czechs was honoured, Benes had him expelled by the police. Further, Benes ensured that Hlinka was arrested on return to his home, on charges of coercion and agitation because of his Paris trip.

On August 20, 1919, the Tusar government gave an order for a census. Although the 1910 census showed that 30% of Northern Hungary's total population was made up of Hungarians (1, 034, 343) and 58% Slovaks (1,686,713), at the peace conference Benes asserted the false figures of 23% and 65% respectively, with 12% being other nationalities. While the 1910 census information was available to the conference delegates, no one appears to have bothered to check Benes' claims. And when Benes, in his three hour speech, tried to justify the Czech demands, no one challenged him. Even when he claimed that there was no need to deal with Slovakia since the joining of the Slovaks and the Czechs was an accomplished fact, still no one spoke. Finally, George Lloyd interrupted him, to ask if Benes' assertion corresponds to the general view, there was no criticism from the conference floor. Clemenceau, the chairman, questioned the delegates and in the end, they voted for a unified Czechoslovakia and the annexation of Northern Hungary to this newly created state.[18] The Allies and Czechoslovakia, on September 10, 1919, signed the agreement of Saint-Germain-an-Lay. In the spirit of the Pittsburg Accord, signed by Masaryk and the American Slovak emigres, it is obvious that this was not the way that the likes of Father Hlinka and General Stefanik envisioned freedom for Slovakians.

CHAPTER 8

Dictated Peace

The purpose of a peace conference is, or should be, to create lasting peace. Real peace comes from security and contentment. These are the prerequisites of the peaceful coexistence of the peoples of the Danubian basin and also of the political, moral and economic reconstruction of Europe.

A great deal of atrocities and injustices have been committed in the pursuit of ideals and ideas. However, history hardly knows of such violations of human freedom as the "peace treaty" of Trianon. At the end of the first world war, well-meaning sociologists and politicians imbued with idealism believed that the victorious and the defeated would meet in their common Christian ideas. Most people seemed to believe that the old Roman principle of "vae victis" (woe to the conquered) had been abandoned, that the victor could no longer maltreat his former foe. When the vanquished peoples surrendered, they put their trust in Wilson's 14 points, in the promise of peace and democracy. As it turned out, the victors took advantage of this trust.

The expansionist designs of the Czechs were promoted by their constant referral to the western democracies. The clique, which seized power in Hungary for a few months, caused political chaos within and generated antipathy in the Allies against the Hungarians. Masaryk and Benes preached democracy and demanded self-government for the Czech and the Slovaks. At the same time they protested against the idea of a referendum. They laid claim to the Sudeten German region, a region which belonged to Austria for centuries, citing the historical right of the Czechs. And at the same time protested against the historical rights claimed by Hungarians over Northern Hungary.

No other nation gained as much as the Czechs after the First World War. All of Northern Hungary was given to them, including Ruthenia The Allies objected to the annexation of Ruthenia by

Russia. The Czechs wanted a common frontier with Rumania. Poland did not lay claim to Ruthenia, so it fell into the hands of Central Europe's most avid nation. The Ruthenians were never consulted. The historical rights of Hungary were completely ignored by the "peacemakers". To be sure, the Allies stipulated that autonomy be given to the Ruthenians, and the Czechs signed an agreement to that effect, but the concordance was never put into effect.

The territorial "adjustment" of Central Europe gave a number of Hungarian-inhabited regions to the neighbouring states. The adjustment was to be based primarily on strategic considerations. The lessons of the Second World War was needed to prove, that "strategic" boundaries are worthless in the face of political and ideological drives.

The dramatic events leading to a historic crescendo can only be evaluated if one follows the events one step at a time:
August 1, 1919, - the "trade-unionists" seized control of the government and established Gyula Peidl as President. On the 3rd, Rumanian occupying forces entered the capitol, Budapest. By the 7th, the party of István Friedrich and András Csilleri forced the abdication of the Peidl-government. Clemenceau refused to recognize the new government, because in his opinion it was not representative of all parties in the country. Clemenceau further objected to the candidature of Prince Joseph for the regency. The ineffective Friedrich government was reshuffled repeatedly.

November 14, - the Rumanians withdrew from the capital and two days later, Miklós Horthy marched in at the head of the Hungarian Army. On the 22nd, Károly Huszár formed a government, which was recognized by the commission of the Allies in Budapest. The Allies invited Huszár to the peace conference.

January 15, 1920, - the Hungarian delegation received, from the Allies, the peace-plan which contained 364 clauses. The following day, Count Albert Apponyi presented the Hungarian perspective and pleaded for a more equitable peace-plan. The powerful arguments of the great

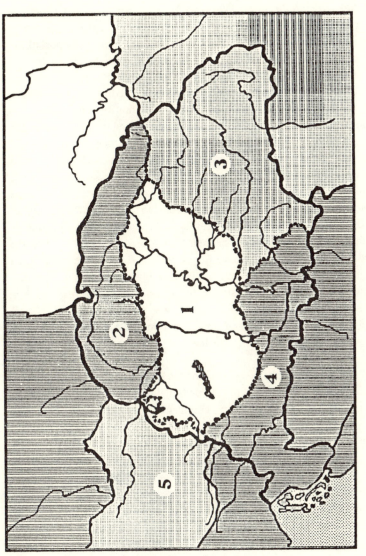

Border re-allocation at Trianon

1. Dismembered Hungary
Hungarian territories attached to
2. Czechoslovakia 3. Romania
4. Yugoslavia 5. Austria

Hungarian could not vie with the already unchallenged misrepresentations of Benes at the conference. During the peace negotiations Benes produced dozens of memorandums in support of the Czech claims. While his advisors worked on the "Czech material" coming from Prague and from the other Czech conspiracy centres. Benes was busy visiting influential politicians and diplomats and giving press conferences in which he discredited the Monarchy and the Hungarian people. He badly needed the assistance of specialists in the composition of his memoranda. Because of time restraints, and growing Allied pressures, statistical data in the memoranda were falsified or invented by the Czech advisors. These memoranda were published by the Czech, because they realized that these records were distortions and fabrications. In the 1930's the Germans obtained copies of the Benes' memoranda and translated, its contents were published in both French and German. The memoranda shed a ghastly light on the birth of Czechoslovakia. Later Benes confessed that those memoranda might contain a few erroneous data, and blamed it on his advisors. However, the Allied delegates to the peace conference believed him without hesitation. No recorded effort was taken to check on Benes' source or on the reliability of his information. Only the military were there, and they saw nothing but the enemy and political chaos.[19]

March 1, 1920, - the suspension of the exercise of Royal Power was proclaimed in Hungary. For a transitional period, the rule by regency was instituted. Miklós Horthy, commander-in-chief of the Hungarian Forces, was elected as the Regent.

May 6, - the Czechoslovak National Assembly elects Tomast B. Masaryk as President of the Republic. Almost immediately, discriminatory practices commence against the Hungarians of Northern Hungary. The Czechoslovak department of Agriculture distributed approximately 3,100,000 acres of land from the expropriated territories of Northern Hungary. Using the portions of properties above the permitted size, 2857 plantations were called into existence: in Slovakia 2054, in Ruthenia 222. In the Czech-Moravian region about 20,000 acres were expropriated, while in Slovakia and Ruthenia more than

60,000 acres were taken from their owners. All the land expropriated came from Hungarian land-owners, without compensation, and was given to Czech, Moravian and Slovak planters.

June 4,   - the Hungarian delegates were forced to sign the dictated peace treaty in the Versailles Palace, Trianon.

And so, History repeated itself! For the Vienna congress of 1814-1815 was convened for the purpose of territorial adjustments. The participating European Powers discussed the question of new state boundaries. The monarchies conquered by Napoleon were restored and consolidated. Metternich was the chairman of the Congress. The agreement signed on the 9th of January, 1815, created a new political situation in Europe. It satisfied the territorial claims of the Great powers and guaranteed the thrones of old Dynasties. France was forced back to its old frontiers. England extended its colonial empire, Russia obtained a good part of Poland, Bessarabia and Finland. Prussia acquired the Rhine provinces plus Poznan, Danzig and part of Saxony. Austria, although lost its territories in Netherlands, gained new ones from Italy and Poland. Germany remained disunited, divided into principalities and monarchies. The Vienna Congress further established an independent Dutch Monarchy, acknowledged the perpetual neutrality of Switzerland, and created a Holy League.

Likewise, the Peace Conference of 1920, in the neighbourhood of Paris created "succession states". The Czech conspiracy and its principal author Benes used the conflict and the resulting Peace Conference to realize their ambitions. Czechoslovakia was not born from a legitimate or even democratic need. The Western fears for the future "security" of Europe was unjustified. Benes, while posing as a champion of peace, made great use of this fear. During the Peace Conference, Benes argued before the delegates, that in order to protect Europe against the German expansion toward the East, Czechoslovakia must have Hungarian cities and territories to be the buffer that the Allies needed against such an expansion. Benes later confessed, that the Hungarian posed question before the conference members, on the existence of Slovakia and proof of its historic borders, worried him greatly. The Czechs and the Moravians were inhabitants of historical countries. But the so called, ancient and long lived, Slovakia was just another fabrication of Benes, "the little Bismarck" of Czechoslovakia.

CHAPTER 9

Future Options

The Trianon Peace Treaty of June 4, 1920, deprived Hungary of three-quarters of its territory and two-thirds of its population. The Hungarian delegates were willing to accept the wishes of the people living in the affected areas. They did not insist on Hungary's historic right, if the inhabitants wished to separate, as a result of a plebiscite. "Let them choose between Hungary and the surrounding countries that want to swallow them on some pretext, let them decide where they wish to belong!", shouted Apponyi in Vienna. The result of a referendum should have been the only deterministic solution to the members of the Trianon Conference. This would have ended once and for all, the territorial hegemony of Central-Europe. Instead, the treaty participants condemned Hungary to dismemberment, as three and a half million Hungarians were severed from their native country. Of those three and a half million Hungarians forced under the domination of foreign powers, some two million lived in the major cities of Pozsony, Kassa, Nagyvárad, Arad, Temesvár and Szabadka. Indeed, for more than three centuries, Pozsony was once the capital of Hungary.

It is a great tragedy, that the decisions made more than seventy years ago resulted in detrimental changes to the ethnography and demography of the Carpathian Basin. In this process, time is on the side of the usurpers. The active and articulate human rights movement only confirms that the succession states practice forced assimilation on their minorities in order to justify their own existence. It is true, that a sensible agreement cannot ignore the current ethnic situation, even though it is the result of a policy which caused forcefully assimilation and resettlement of minorities. However, a future referendum, which must occur, cannot accept the status quo; the fruit of an old injustice. If future conflicts are to be deterred, such as Yugoslavia and perhaps even Czechoslovakia, an acceptable formula must be found. In what other way can a perpetuate peace be realized in Central and Eastern Europe?

At the present, the boundaries of Trianon are but fuel to the minorities in their endless struggle for autonomy. No one can doubt, that had the plebescite been held in 1920, today's ethnic violence would not exist. As an example, where people were given their say, as in Schleswig-Holstein, Sopron and Saar-land, no one has since disputed the validity of those borders.

Hungarians understand that, however painful it is, the restoration of the thousand year old Hungary is now but a dream. However, a United Nations Task Force should be commissioned to evaluate boundary readjustment claims, based on plebescite, for all disputed areas and adjudicate a frontier re-adjustment program. Should at a later date, the confederation of Danubian states be realized, the gradual fading of frontiers and the increase of mutual trade would certainly alleviate the pain caused by the adjustments. The ideal solution, in the words of Coudenhove-Klergie, would be, "the disappearance of the boundaries between countries", Without the initial frontier re-adjustments, it would be futile to expect harmony in Central Europe, because autonomy is considered a fundamental right by the inhabitants. It is hard to conceive the easing of century-old tensions any other way.

In 1937 Sir Robert Gower, a member of the House of Commons in England, speaking on the great injustice against Hungary, said:

> "In our view, prosperity cannot be expected in that part of Europe until the antagonism and rancour characterizing the relation of the peoples to one another are eliminated. It cannot be in the interest of any state or people to maintain conditions that are opposed to fairness, making trade impossible. This situation may threaten the peace of the world."

He continued: "It is a matter of returning the regions inhabited by Hungarians all along the present frontiers. And wherever several nationalities live together, there should be a referendum, for peoples have a right for self determination. An adjustment of this nature would benefit all. it would lesson the number of minorities groups and heal a great deal of discontent. For the equilibrium of Central Europe, the revision of the peace treaties is essential. Harmony and order must take the place of chaos and hate."

Nitti Francesco, former Prime Minister of Italy, wrote this in the thirties:

"No one can be at ease, while in the possession of a thing acquired through injustice. For this reason the succession states have lived in fear since Trianon, afraid of revisions and revenge. This fear will persist until they agree to the re-shaping of Central Europe."

Unfortunately, in the last seventy odd years, there has not been one Central or Eastern European State, which willing gave up even a small portion of its acquisitions. The only two exceptions were, when compelled by the Vienna decrees of November, 1938, and of August, 1940. On the contrary, they loudly protested the demands for the return of land and people belonging to former states, such as Hungary. Further, these states, such as Czechoslovakia, Rumania and Yugoslavia, equally object to international protestation against their systematic oppression of Hungarian and other minorities within their borders. Decades have gone by and the fate of these minorities have not improved. For example; in Transylvania and Northern Hungary, where the oppressive measures have become progressively unbearable. Gyula Zathureczky, an expert in Eastern European Affairs, eloquently stated that;

"The minorities living in Eastern Europe are silenced. They have no means of defending themselves. Their de-nationalization and de-culturalization has progressed fast under the communist regimes, especially during the last four decades, when they could rely neither on the support of international organizations nor on that of the government in Hungary. Moreover, the traditionally outspoken churches are now suppressed or paralyzed. Our brethren living in the neighbouring countries are subjected to political harassment and persecution."

The government of the succession states expect that their minorities will get tired of those harassments and their policy of assimilation will succeed. We hope it will never happen. So for the struggle of Hungarians in northern Hungary and Transylvania, their struggle for survival has been miraculous. But we cannot overlook the fact that their numbers are ever dwindling. When time comes for the reshaping of Central Europe, we have to be realistic, we have to make allowance for the ethnographic changes, but not at the expense of the human rights of individuals. Any federation or confederation would come to a failure unless equality before the law is enjoyed by all. This is the only possible conclusion drawn from the last seventy or so years, when Czechs and Slovaks, Serbians and Croatians were compelled to live together in constant tension.

"In theory, it would not be difficult to rebuild Central Europe", wrote Tibor Eckhardt in 1934. His proposals were based on the principals advocated by the Allies:

1.) A degree of national unity is the first requirement. In the case of Hungary, it would be necessary to return large areas along the frontier to the mother land. This in turn would ease the tension in the surrounding countries.

2.)   The self-determination of the people is another must. It would enable the Croatians, Slovaks and Ruthenians, to mention a few, to decide whether they want to be independent or partners in the country of their choice.

3.)   The gradual transformation of Central Europe is highly desirable if not inevitable. Initially, a confederation should be formed with the participation of Austria, Hungary and Czechoslovakia. It would become the foundation-stone of the equilibrium in Europe. The final objective would be the co-operation of the peoples from the Baltic to the Adriatic and Black Sea.

Today it is quite clear that the countries along the Danube need one another, that their hostilities in the past profited no one except the great powers. Some day they must join forces, it is in their common interest

As the historian George Roux remarks, "the tragedy of these people is that politically they can't get along and economically they cannot thrive without one another. The reconciliation of Danubian nations is demanded by their geographic location." But to arrive at this reconciliation, they have to be fully aware of their common interests and be willing to make concessions. Here we have to repeat that one of the fundamental faults of the Trianon pease treaty was the destruction of the economic integrity of the former Hungary.

Along the Danube, many people are turning to the idea of 'Regional Federation'. Yugoslavia was held together by brute ethnic force, and as a result it is in the painful process of shattering. The Czechoslovak crisis of 1968 provided the Slovaks with an opportunity to assert their equality and their wish to be independent. Such movements and endeavour corresponded to the fundamental requirements of Central Europe. So the situation creates by the Soviet Union after the second world war cannot be considered final. The same factors and forces, that caused the dissolution of the Austro-Hungarian Monarchy, are now at work in the successive states.

Hungarians dare to hope, that their neighbours are already awakening to a common interests and that the conditions for reconciliation are now better than they were before the second world war. Successive states should understand that the settlement of territorial disputes is the first step toward this reconciliation. It is needless to say, that there is a great difference between Hungary before the Second World War and Hungary today. This equally applies to the surrounding countries too. The latest generation did not live through the traumas of two wars, nor do they have the prejudices and grudges their parents and grandparents had, therefore, they are more disposed to compromises. The old hate stirred up by propaganda has faded, for many, in the last decades. There is still the new hate of the passing communistic oppression. The Yugoslavian struggle is a remnant of the decade old communist power struggle between its ethnic ruling classes and the rest of their minorities. Once that fades as well, future negotiations will be done in a more congenial atmosphere. After the age of burning and blind passion, common sense will prevail.

Hungary is situated in the heart of Europe. Without its participation, no political or economic revival can occur. The prosperity of Central Europe depends on the co-operation of its nations. Jacque Bainville, a man of prophetic insight, said in 1920, right after Hungary was dismembered:

> "In that part off Europe the effective federalizing element will be not the most populace but the strongest nation, the one that is able to unite them all...the Hungarian appears to be the one, for it has a deep national consciousness and a firm will, unlike its neighbours. It is the purest in Central Europe. The Great Powers should not hinder its rise and progress. No matter how small, the Hungarian nation occupies the central position in the Danubian Basin and its role is found to be significant."

Hungary's more than seventy year old claim for territorial adjustment is justified by the present turn of events in Central and Eastern Europe. The burning minority problems, which are the consequences of a misguided peace treaty dictated by prejudice and distrust, speak for themselves. Now that the principles of the 1956 freedom-fighting has been realized, Hungary can again raise its voice in leadership and urge her neighbours to exercise the principle of minority self determination, as signed in the Trianon Peace Treaty, and call on the international community to correct the past wrongs by monitoring and supporting minorities in their human rights struggle.

To quote the late Benedictine monk, Jeromos Szalay, whose work was published in 1957:

> "The happiness of a people, as of an individual, cannot be built upon the misery of others, nor can a nation be sentenced to death to ensure the survival of another. The demands of rights and justice are universal. Every nation believes in its own truth and defends it as if it were absolute truth. Some persons are so blind by their national selfishness that they ignore the rights of others. We should try to clarify all problems in the spirit of mutuality, with respect for all involved. Let us unite the Danubian peoples in the spirit of understanding and reconciliation."

All that has been said or quoted above in regard to Trianon and Hungary, bears upon the future of Northern Hungary, which is an organic part of the Carpathian Basin and of Hungary.

FOOTNOTES:

(PART II)

1. A Double Conquest of the Homeland (A Kettös Honfoglallás) Gyula László, Budapest, 1978, Magvetö, page 22.

2. The demography of Hungary. The population distribution of Hungary from the homeland settlement to 1949 (Magyarország történeti demografiája. Magyarország népessége a Honfoglalástol 1949-ig) Jozsef Kovacsics, Budapest, Közgazdasági és Jogi Könyvkiadó, 1963, Panoráma, 1977, page 164.

3. The Attila Trilogy (Attila-trilógia), Egyed Rudnay, Author's Edition, Brussels, 1964,Volume 1, Page 21.

4. The Larousse Encyclopedia, Paris, 1976.

5. Evaluation of Central Europe, Stuttgart, 1970.

6. Political Works of Carl Marx (Marx Károly politikia munkái), Volume 6, Budapest, 1960, page 196.

7. In the footsteps of the Árpáds (Az Árpádok nyomában), Dezsö Dümmerth, Second Edition, Budapest, Panoráma, 1977, page 164.

8. Those historic confession were first published by the Délamerikai Magyar Hirlap (South American Hungarian News magazine) towards the end of the Fifties. This series of articles were later reprinted in the form of a book. The author used the code-name "Nemo". Detail of the "Czech Conspiracy" and its operation are detailed in these articles.

9. Hungarian-Slav Accord (Magyar-Szlovak kiegyezés), István Borsody, Budapest, 1928, Page 82.

10. This was the author's personal experience in Northern Hungary. As the son of a railway man and with two older brothers also railway employees, he and his family personally seen the people and goods traffic in this area .

11. The Károlyi indictment took place at the express order of the Allies.

126

12. Hungarian Historic Chronology (Magyar Történelmi Kronologia), Peter Gunst, Second Edition, Budapest, Tankönyvkiado, 1970, page 319.

Note: The National Council proclaimed a plebiscitary decision consisting of five clauses, which asserted "the independence of the Republic of Hungary". The following day, November 17, 1918, Béla Kun and his group of communists, trained in Russia, arrived in Budapest.

13. Horthy Diary (Emlékirataim), Miklós Horthy, Second Edition, Toronto, Vörösváry-Weller Publishing Co. Ltd., 1974, pages 108-109.

14. Béla Linder - is mentioned by the 1918 Army List as an artillery lieutenant colonel. In the "Révai NagyLexikon", however, he appears as "a former staff-colonel", page 569.

15. Benes, István Borsody, Budapest, Athenaeum, 1936, page 66.

16. Hungarian pages (Magyar füzetek), 4. Paris, 1982, page 76.

17. Benes, Ibid, page 68.

18. Ibid, page 75.

19. Hungarian Historic Chronology (Magyar Történelmi Kronologia), Peter Gunst, Second Edition, Budapest, Tankönyvkiado, 1970, page 322.

Note: Possibly the only exception was the team headed by the American professor Archibald Cery Coolidge, an expert in Central European history. The team was sent to the Central European countries to collect data. On january 19, 1919, Coolidge sent his report on Hungary to President Wilson. He strongly recommended the preservation of the economic unity of Hungary and objected to the annexation of Transylvania. He considered that support for the Károlyi - regime was necessary in order to check the spread of communism. His opinion, that the integrity and unity of the Carpathian Basin should be left intact, was unheeded by the members of the Versailles Peace Conference.

PART III.

THE FATE OF THE MINORITY

CHAPTER 1

The First Czechoslovak Republic
1918 - 1938

The United States Government, on May 29, 1918 ratified the declaration made by the "oppressed minorities" at their Rome gathering. A few days later, the Allied War Council, meeting on June 3 at Versailles, also endorsed the minorities agreement. The first to officially recognize the new Czechoslovak Republic was France, on June 29, followed by Great Britain on August 9, and the United States on September 3. On October 14, 1918, before the Allied War Council and the treaty conference members, Edward Benes announced the formation of a Czechoslovak government and joined the Allies against the Austro-Hungarian and German Triumvirate.

The Provisional Czechoslovak Government, on October 28, 1918, proclaimed the establishment of the Republic
The first National Assembly consisted of 270 members, whose deputies were appointed. No German or Hungarian minority member received a seat in the new parliament. The assembly unanimously elected Masaryk as their President and appointed Kramar as the Prime Minister, Benes as Minister of Foreign Affairs, and Stefanik as War Minister. On December 21, Masaryk quickly returned to Prague, to be inaugurated as President the very next day.

Masaryk and Benes advocated to the international community, that the model of their state would be fashioned after the likeness of Switzerland. As their future actions proved it, this was far from their intent. The foreign policies of Czechoslovakia were misleading, as its internal policies were oppressive. Its weapon against its minorities was terror and intimidation almost from the start. The governing body of Czechoslovakia was brought about, not by democratic means, but by self serving appointments and biased adjudication. The New Order for the region had one obvious purpose, and that was 'Slavonification of the non-Slav population'.

Czechoslovakia, established on the St. Germain and Trianon Treaty precepts, had 13,612,000 inhabitants. Of these, 6,299,000 were Czech-Moravians and 7,313,000 were of other minority origin. And yet, in the 1918 assembly the majority seats were appointed to Czech nationalists and only 44 seats were given to cooperative Slovaks. The Slovak leaders, who demanded autonomy on the strength of the Pittsburg agreement, were ignored. The Czechoslovak Parliamentary was not only at odds with their much publicized Swiss model, but their procedures and methods were biased, to say the least. As an example, a Slav oriented bill required 19,000 votes for ratification, while a non-Slav "minority oriented" proposal required 27,000 votes.[1]

At the time of the First Assembly, government control amounted to a selective form of martial law. The press was under censorship and travelling was restricted. The loyalty of the citizenry was overseen by the 'Propaganda Kancellaria' (State Security Department). Suspects were arrested without warrants and ethnic group meetings were prohibited. Not a shred of democracy was evident. Further more, areas inhabited by Hungarians and Slovaks were given colonial status. The rising domestic tension eventually manifested itself in a steelworker' strike. The Czech police responded with brutality and bullets. The Hungarian minority were blamed for the strike, even though, seventy five percent of the steel workers participating in the Korpona strike were Slovaks. Those Hungarians, who participated in the strike were imprisoned, while the non-participating Hungarian company employees were forcibly evicted and deposited at the Hungarian border. While internationally claiming religious neutrality, the Czechoslovak government next attacked the religious fibre of the Catholic Hungarian majority. Demonstrating its religious 'tolerance' and singular brand of democracy, the government expelled from Czechoslovakia the five Hungarian bishops, namely; Vilmos Batthyány of Nyitra, Sándor Párvy of Szepes, Farkas Radnay of Besztercebánya, István Novák of Eperjes and Antal Papp of Munkács, who administered to the spiritual needs of their people.

Two other drastic methods used, to de-nationalize ethnic Hungarians and other minorities, were the falsification of demographic statistics and the introduction of discriminatory school policies. According to the 1910 census, 1,069.978 Hungarians lived in Northern Hungary. Of those Hungarians, a total of 106,840 were expelled from Czechoslovakia by 1924. However, the 1921 Czechoslovak enumeration only showed 744,620, while the 1930 census accounted for 719,569 Hungarians within the borders of Czechoslovakia. [2] That the official census figures were not correct is evident simply because in the 1935 Czechoslovak Parliamentary elections the two Hungarian parties received 234,943 votes. Another proof was that after the return of Northern Hungary in 1941, the Hungarian census found 892,677 Hungarians in the reannexed area, although many more Hungarians remained under Czechoslovakian rule.[3]

Between 1918 and 1938 the handling of the "school problem" appeared to be somewhat liberal. In reality, severe anti-democratic and anti-minority measures were taken. In 1918, 3,641 elementary schools were operating in northern Hungary. The language was Hungarian in 3,298 of them, German or Slovak in 343. In 1937, Hungarian was taught in as few as 754 schools in Slovakia and in 121 schools in Ruthenia. (The number of pupils was 85,507 in Slovakia, 16,515 in Ruthenia.) A total of 1,860 teachers were teaching. They had to retain the language in these schools for the children spoke only Hungarian. The intention to assimilate the Hungarian minority was most obvious on the high school level. Out of 60 Hungarian high schools only 8 remained. In the universities of Czechoslovak not a single Hungarian professor received a teaching position.

The ethnic distribution of the Danubian basin is so entangled that it is next to impossible to draw borders satisfying all. This circumstance, however, does not justify putting large, overwhelmingly Hungarian areas under foreign rule. The Trianon peace-treaty separated more than a quarter of the Hungarians from their motherland. This created stress not only in Hungary, but in all the surrounding succession states. While Czechoslovakia provided homes for 97% of its people, Rumania for 96%, Yugoslavia for 93%, only 74% of the European Hungarians were allowed to live in the land of their ancestors.[4] After the First World War, about a hundred thousand torn-away Hungarians left everything and fled South of the Danube. In time, some 350,000 returned from the surrounding states and resettled in Hungary. Still, more than two and a half million remained outside the Hungarian border. There were few families in Hungary proper, who did not have relatives living in the annexed areas attached to other countries.[5] The bulk of refugees tried to settle in cities and towns. There was an acute housing shortage. Thousands of families lived in botchy barracks or else in idle wagons at railway stations for months.

Trianon also deprived Hungary of most of its natural resources. The country ran into poverty and debts. As a result, between the two wars, revisionism and irredentism became dominant political platforms. Facts blown out of proportion by foreign propaganda, served to antagonize the people in the succession states and the fate of their Hungarian minorities became more and more unbearable. The Hungarian people were not responsible for the Central European catastrophe. István Tisza, as Prime Minister of Hungary, strongly opposed the Monarchy's declaration of war. The Czech, Masaryk, for opportunistic political gains blamed Hungary for the war, which it did not start. But it did not stop here. After the First World War, even before the ink dried on the documents of the Trianon Peace Treaty, the discrimination began. The agreement over the protection of minorities made between the Allies and Czechoslovakia, which intended to assure the equality of all citizens before the law, was quickly ignored by the Czechoslovak government. It reserved the right to deal with the minorities in its own way.

Czechoslovakia continued a foreign policy to ensure the isolation of Hungary. Because, the principal objective of the Allies was the constraint of Germany, they subordinated all other matters, including the Czech demands. This circumstance caused great anxiety for Benes. With a shrewd turn, he proclaimed that the Carpathian Basin was a key territory of high strategic importance and that Hungary was the greatest threat to the Western Alliance. "They must be bound hand and foot", he insisted, "Let the Czechs tackle this problem". Hungary was "terra incognita" on the map, at least for some Western politicians. They knew it as a part of the Habsburg Empire. Benes himself had never been in Hungary, however, he was firmly resolved to wipe it off the map. As a result of his international and domestic propaganda campaign, the Czechs in general came to mistrust all Hungarians and were made to see them as rivals on the Central European scene. Bismarck had once remarked, that "He who rules the Czechs, rules the rest of Europe". Benes, filled with personal ambitions, wanted to become the chancellor of Central Europe. What Benes failed to remember was, that Bismarck had seen Hungary in an important role, that of a bulwark against Eastern invasions. Whereas, to the Czech politicians, Hungary was a competitor with interests opposed to their own.

The Western European economists and the diplomats of the League of Nations were aware of the economic interdependence of all nations in Central Europe. Benes, who spent months in Geneva, untiringly lobbying against all plans that would have raised Hungary from its isolation, was quick to put the labels "irredentism" or "revisionism" on those plans. This time, instead of producing his own plans at the Paris Peace Talks, he secured the services of Andre Tardieu, an advisor to Clemenceau. Tardieu presented a lengthy dissertation on "The Economic Status of the Danubian States" before the members of the conference. The essence of his presentation was supported by Nicolae Titulescu, the head of the Rumanian delegation in Geneva. Titulescu was a firm believer in the obscure theory of the "spiritualization" of the political frontiers. Both of them opposed any border revision to the lines of demarcation. The Hungary was willing to co-operate but insisted on the re-adjustment of its boundaries. Benes, the extreme nationalist accused Hungary of narrow mindedness and chauvinism. The Rumanians, on the other hand envisioned a "Great Rumania" and refused to return any land which was now in their possession.

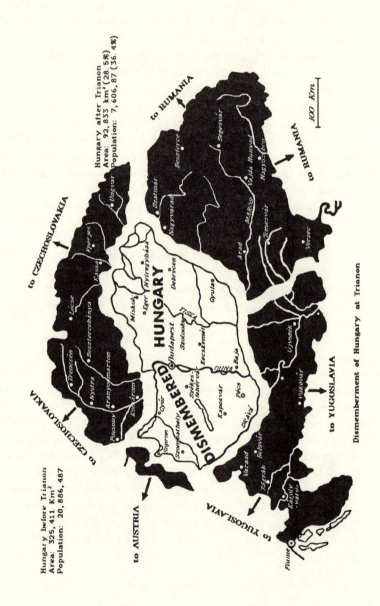

Hungary before Trianon
Area: 325,411 Km²
Population: 20,886,487

Hungary after Trianon
Area: 92,833 km²(28.5%)
Population: 7,606,87 (36.4%)

Dismemberment of Hungary at Trianon

to CZECHOSLOVAKIA

to CZECHOSLOVAKIA

to RUMANIA

to RUMANIA

to AUSTRIA

to YUGOSLAVIA

to YUGOSLAVIA

DISMEMBERED

HUNGARY

100 Km

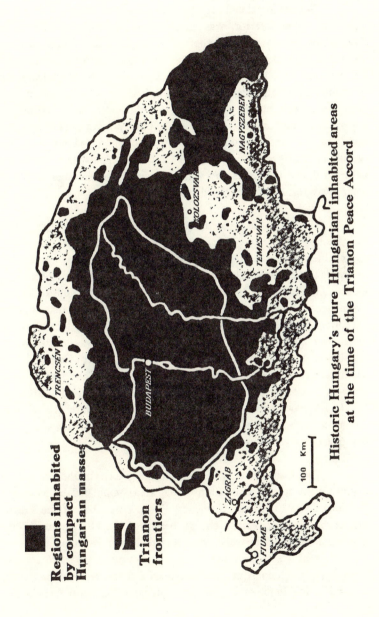

Regions inhabited
by compact
Hungarian masses

Trianon
frontiers

Historic Hungary's pure Hungarian inhabited areas
at the time of the Trianon Peace Accord

100 Km

TRENCSÉN

BUDAPEST

KOLOZSVÁR

NAGYSZEBEN

TEMESVÁR

ZÁGRÁB

FIUME

Part III

The despoiled and impoverished Hungary, shaken by its own bolshevik reign of terror, was on the brink of economic ruin. The Czechs saw this. Since the import of wheat from the Hungarian Plain was vital to Slovakia, Benes supported the League of Nations' financial aid program for Hungary. However, he refused to acknowledge the need for frontier adjustments. In vain did Albert Apponyi prove, that permanent reconciliation and lasting peace could be achieved not by papers that sanctions the "status quo", but by a reasonable and just distribution of land and goods. Benes was not interested in justice. He wanted to reinforce the new state of Czechoslovakia with treaties. He believed that if the status quo was maintained long enough, it would wear away resistance and breed resignation.

The Czechs demanded the democratization of Hungary, while the Czechoslovakian government violated the principles of democracy against their minorities. To mention a few examples: they confiscated the lands that exceeded 200 cadastral acres, without any compensation, then redistributed the expropriated lands to Czech and Moravian claimants. Slovaks received only limited share and that was by exception, while Hungarians received no land at all. The locally owned Hungarian manufacturing and industrial sector was curtailed by legislation to the point, where it was no longer financially or economically viable to operate. They forced the children of civil servants to attend Czech schools. Through the use of administrative and legislative means, the Hungarian intellectuals were driven from Czechoslovakia, while the remaining Hungarian middle class was driven to impoverishment.

The Hungarians within Czechoslovakia remained united in deploring the fateful annexation of the areas populated by Magyars. On June 2, 1920, Lajos Körmendy Ékes, a member of the Prague parliament, read a declaration, on behalf of the Hungarian and the German minorities, in which he stated that their participation in the legislation of Czechoslovakia served one purpose, to raise protests against the grave constitutional injustices and the deprivation of their civil rights.[6] In the same year, on September 24, Jozsef Szent-Ivány,

138

another member of parliament uttered there words: "We have never approved the peace treaty. Nor shall we ever abandon our claim for self determination. We are compelled to live as citizens of Czechoslovakia, however. Our present task is to secure our human existence in this territory."[7] Such an acceptance of the fait accompli was characteristic of the Hungarian minority, which remained faithful to its own nationality and culture. The older generation of Northern Hungarians spoke some Slovak. Those who were forced to attend Czech schools learned the state language, went to universities, but at home, in the Church, in clubs, where ever they could, they used the language of their fathers and clung to their traditions. As a response to the nationalistic feelings of the misplaced Hungarians of Northern Hungarian, their Czechoslovak citizenship status was left in abeyance. While in 1920, the Czechoslovak government readily bestowed citizenship status on the German and Austrian minorities, for a long time to come, they refused to extend citizenship privilege to the Hungarian minority. When they did enact citizenship laws, it was to facilitate deportation. The result was, as the 1930 census revealed, that there were 26,646 Hungarians in Czechoslovakia who were considered "stateless".

CHAPTER 2

Versailles and Trianon

The Versailles and Trianon Peace Treaties were dictated terms and conditions, worked out by the Paris Council of the Peace Conference. Through the council's arbitrary territorial adjustments, which fundamentally stemmed from fear of German reprisal, the seeds of discord, discontent and future wars were sown. The chief political architects, Tardieu, Briand and Clemenceau, allowed their concerns, fears and social theories to influence a peace settlement, which could have ended all protracted antagonisms. At Trianon, arbitration was hardly a concern, quarrel over the spoils was. The non conciliatory atmosphere of the conference, provided the Pan-Slav movement with a green light. Its principal promoters, Masaryk and Benes, took every advantage to promote their ideas to members of the conference. Their successful courtship influenced the Allies in such a way, as to endorse the so called 'slavic style' of arbitration, in which millions of people, whose defeated governments were judged at Trianon, were brought under Slav domination. The Wilson doctrine, urging "liberation from oppression", showed clear signs of Masaryk and Benes influences, for the Pan-Slav union was but a dream before the First World War. It certainly became a reality between the two World Wars, at least in the form of a common ideology and political aims. It did not mature under the protective wings of a Russian Tzar, rather it flourished in the Pan-Slav embracing, world domineering design of a Bolshevik begotten Soviet Russia.

The Great Powers, dictating the terms of peace, did not foresee any danger from the Soviet Union at the time. They believed that the Bolsheviks under Lenin had enough internal problems to deal with. But, before long, Litvinov, a member of the Soviet Foreign Ministry, informed Stalin that in the divided Central Europe, Russia may find friendship, support and acceptance amongst the Slavic succession states. Hungary, wedged in between the Northern and Southern Slavs, debilitated by war and mutilation, could easily be absorbed or even liquidated. As Stalin said, this was only a question of wagons. The French were afraid of a German revenge, while the Czechs were afraid of the revisionist movement. The Great Powers did not see, or did not want to see, the masterly moves of the Soviets on the diplomatic chess board, The small Slavic people became the pawns in the game of East versus West.

A divided Europe was the tragic legacy of Versailles. The peoples, deprived of their freedom and deeply humiliated, tried to break out of their isolation, of course. Their lot became unbearable, because of their isolation, helplessness and the brutality of their oppressors. Benes, the President of the Czechoslovak Republic, once pointedly remarked to the Hungarian Ambassador, "If you do not abandon your revisionist policy, I'll hound you to hell!"[8] Sumner Welles, the American Deputy Secretary of State, called Germany and Hungary "the bandit nations"[9]. And, Winston Churchill considered the German, Italian and Hungarian politicians as nothing more than "desperados"[10]. In his book, "The Time for Decision" (Washington, 1944), Sumner Welles speaks of Hungarians as "beasts of prey", and as "the hyenas of the unfortunate Czechoslovaks". Such Western ignorance and animosity not only provided the fuel for future smoldering discontent, but opened the taps of Communism to permeate and poison the states of Central and Eastern Europe.

Shortly after the First World War and the ratification of the treaties, the League of Nations was conceived and formed by the victorious Allied nations. The 1919 Paris Peace Conference formulated its charter, which was inserted in the texts of the peace pacts. The League was to promote the co-operation of nations and thus, international peace and security. With its headquarters in Geneva, Switzerland, the League enthusiastically encouraged all nations to join. Included among its members were the victors, the neutral states and the vanquished. Hungary, too, became a member in 1922 and stayed until 1938. The League, to exercise its charter, had three organs: the General Assembly, the Council and the Secretariat. Its very composition prevented the fulfilment of its primary task. For unanimity of decision was required in every important question, and unanimity was next to impossible to achieve. Ironically, while most of the vanquished states joined the international organization, the United States decided not to participate and the Soviet Union did not become a member until 1934.

The League of Nations, although it included the vanquished states, its policies soon came to reflect the views and the will of England and France. The demand for the disarmament of the conquered nations and the retention of the status quo became the dominant theme of the League. The discontent of those, who had suffered injustice and the emerging revisionism, created tension. The influence of the Little Entente, especially that of Czechoslovakia and Rumania, grew strong. To gain domestic and international freedom, Germany and Japan withdrew from the League in 1933. In 1934, when the Soviet Union joined the League, the character of the organization changed and the Slavic influence became even stronger. The disregard of the rules of fairness was bound to bring about at last, the disintegration of the League of Nations. Hungary frustrated and demoralized left the League in 1938. The invasion of Finland by the Soviet Union in 1939, underlined the utter impotence of the League. Unable to prevent a war, for which it was originally formed for, the League of Nations officially dissolved in 1946.

The Peace Treaty Disarmament Orders were soon to hamstrung the governments of the vanquished nations. The treaty required the disarmament of the victorious and vanquished nations alike, for the sake of international peace. Few believed, that the victors would keep to the spirit and practice of the multilateral disarmament agreement. For the vanquished, all offensive weapons were prohibited. Germany's military strength was reduced to 100,000 soldiers and Hungary's and Austria's was limited to 35,000. Hardly adequate to maintain internal order. On the other hand, without limitation on size, the armies of the victors surrounding Germany were being equipped with the most modern offensive weapons of the time. Counted amongst the victors, the armies of the Little Entente surrounding Hungary were allowed to increase their military strength to 540,000 servicemen and their air arsenal to 3,000 airplanes.[11] This large scale rearmament was meant to intimidate the Hungarians, who were filled with anti-

Soviet feelings after the nightmare of the first proletarian dictatorship. The creation of Versailles, the League of Nations, which rigorously supervised the disarmament of the conquered nations, turned a blind eye to the continued arming of the victors. The Allied League members failed to deal with the most portentous outcome of their action, which resulted in the profound ideological and economical transformation of Central Europe. Tragically, one such result of their neglect was the drastic lowering of the living standards for the Czechoslovakian Hungarian minority middle class. As an example, one of the first activities of the Czechoslovak Government, in the name of national security, was the replacement of all Hungarians in government service, without compensation or opportunity for redress, by Czech and Slovak nationalists. Because of this, and other Czechoslovak Minority Policies, many of these people lost their subsistence, causing the virtual collapse of a layer of society, which was European in its civilization, culture, and view of life.

CHAPTER 3

German Protectorate
Independent Slovakia

Addressing the political committee of the League of Nations on September 23, 1938, Litvinov, Soviet Commissar, declared that the Soviet-Czechoslovak Pact could only take effect if France pledged its active co-operation in the pact. The Soviet Union, at the same time, warned Poland, that violation of the Czechoslovak border would result in the nullification of the non-aggressions pact between their two countries. Three days later, Hitler was informed that England, France and the Soviet Union have come to an agreement on the Czechoslovak question. The American President, Roosevelt, distressed over deteriorating international relations, expressed his concerns in a communique to the European governments. During a mass rally in Berlin, Hitler in his address seriously criticized Benes and his government. As a result, the possibility of reconciliation between Germany and Czechoslovakia vanished, in spite of the repeated intervention by Roosevelt. The threat of war became more and more real. Sensing the winds of discord, and in order to try to defuse the volatile international situation, Chamberlain announced in the House of Commons his intention to meet Hitler, Mussolini and Daladier in Munich. The meeting of the 'Big Four' took place on the September 29, 1938. During the conference they agreed that Czechoslovakia must hand over the Sudeten German areas to Germany, and this was to be done before the October 10. Because the Hungarian Government had repeatedly protested, to Prague and the international community, against the unprovoked Czechoslovak military escalation along her borders, the participants of the Munich conference decided that the Hungarian and Polish minority question and border dispute with Czechoslovakia were to be resolved within the next three months.

The Munich Summit participants having ratified German claims on the Sudetenland, ordered Czechoslovakia to return the 28,706 square kilometre area, inhabited by three and a half million people, to Germany. On October 1, 1938, German troops began the occupation of the Sudetenland. Trying to take advantage of the new situation in Prague, Slovak autonomist like Matus Csernák, the Minister of Slovak Affairs, in an extra ordinary council meeting, demanded complete autonomy for Slovakia. The Prime Minister, Jan Syrovy, immediately forwarded the ultimatum to Benes, who refused even a reply. The infuriated Csernák resigned and left Prague. Like wise, Benes, on October 5, recognizing the winds of storm, also resigned and promptly moved to London. Soon after the resignation and departure of Benes, the Czech Government announced the formation of the Czechoslovak National Unity Party, which was immediately joined by the Czech Fascist Party. The Central Government in short order introduced a declaration regulating the relationship between Slovakia and the rest of the State, and tentatively offered Karolsidor, the representative of the Autonomous Slovak Government, a position as Minister without portfolio. There was but one stipulation made by the Czechoslovak Central Government. It demanded an oath of allegiance from the Autonomous Slovak Government. The Slovaks rejected the demand immediately. At the orders of Syrovy, Prime Minister of the Czechoslovak Central Government, the Besztercebánya Army Corps was mobilized and directed to occupy the Vág valley, Pozsony and Zsolna. On March 10, 1939, a State of Emergency was declared in the breakaway state of Slovakia. Slovak autonomists armed the police squads of the Hlinka-Guards, which resulted in a bloody anti-Hungarian demonstration in Pozsony.

Tiso, the President of the breakaway Slovakia, sent Hitler a report on Czechoslovakian internal affairs and offered Hitler the support of his Slovak Government for a certain recompense. On March 13, 1939, a meeting was arranged amongst Hitler, Ribbentrop and Tiso, during which they came to   agree on the secession of Slovakia from the Czechoslovak Republic. The following day, the Slovak Parliament in Pozsony proclaimed the independence of Slovakia. Not to be left out, Emil Hacha, the successor of Benes, and Frantisek Chualkovsky, the Czechoslovak Foreign Minister in order to ensure favoured status, signed an agreement in Berlin, which made Bohemia and Moravia a German Protectorate. The German occupation of Bohemia and Moravia went without any resistance. And, on March 15,

1939, Hitler himself marched into Prague to the enthusiastic welcome of tens of thousands Hitler announced to the cheering Czechs, that Germany was taking charge of the defense of their country. Tiso, also wanting under the German umbrella, requested Hitler's protection for Slovakia. Two days later, with the approval of the Slovak Parliament in Pozsony, German troops occupied Slovakia, all the way to the West of the Vág river.

The newly independent Slovak government was fearful of a Hungarian minority, which numbered over a third of the total population. To legitimize Slovak power in the government, their first decree on March 20, 1939, was to reduce to one seat the Hungarian ethnic representation in the Slovak Parliament. With this dictatorial move, Slovakia virtually became a one-party fascist state. Hitler intending to create a German province out of Slovakia and Hungary, ignored the Hungarian minority objections in Slovakia, instead, for the Tiso government compliance, Hitler guaranteed Slovak independence for twenty-five years.

The Poles, who watched the Czech and Slovak love affair with Germany unfold, did so with growing anxiety. The Polish press claimed, that Slovakia, a newly formed nation of two and a half million people, threatened and in fact attacked Poland, a millennial state with a population of over thirty million. Poland demanded border re-adjustment. The Hungarian government equally concerned, wanted the Slovaks to evacuate Ruthenia, where a political vacuum has developed. Instead, Slovakia laid claim to Ruthenia as its own and to create a "fait accompli", it engaged in partisan activities against Ruthenians and Hungarians alike. In response, Hungarian troops advanced into the region to restore peace and order. The Slovakian retaliation, on March 23, came in the form of an air raid against the city of Ungvár. A swift Hungarian counter air strike brought the hostility to a conclusion, and on April 4, 1939, the two adversaries signed a pact, in which the eastern borders of Slovakia was clearly established.

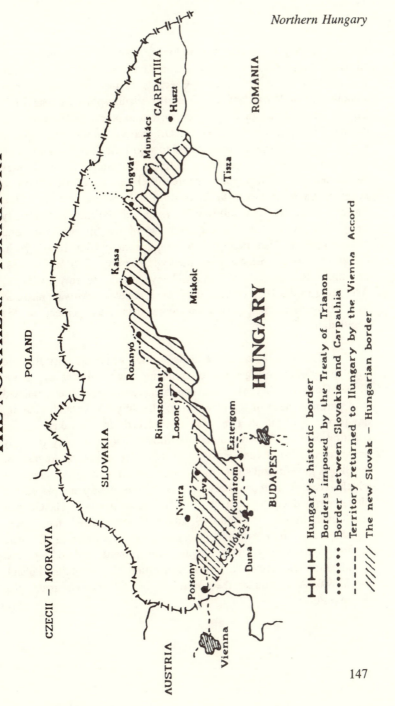

HUNGARY IN 1938 AFTER THE RETURN OF THE NORTHERN TERRITORY

Northern Hungary

POLAND

CZECH – MORAVIA

SLOVAKIA

AUSTRIA

Vienna

Pozsony

Nyitra

Léva

Csallóköz

Komárom

Duna

Esztergom

BUDAPEST

Losonc

Rimaszombat

Rozsnyó

Kassa

Miskolc

Ungvár

Munkács

Huszt

CARPATHIA

HUNGARY

ROMANIA

Tisza

┼┼┼ Hungary's historic border

──── Borders imposed by the Treaty of Trianon

•••• Border between Slovakia and Carpathia

---- Territory returned to Hungary by the Vienna Accord

///// The new Slovak – Hungarian border

147

In Prague, the German military order was replaced by civil administration. Hitler appointed Baron Konstantin Neurath, a former Foreign Minister, as Protector of Czech-Moravia. The transition was smooth. Most Slovak and Czech civil servants spoke German well. Equally, a good part of the railway system in Northern Hungary was owned by Austrian concerns. Originally, before the Vienna Conferences, the negotiators intended to adjust the disputed borders on the basis of the 1910 census. But, by November 2, 1938, they abandoned the original plan, apparently, because of Tiso's visit to Munich, where he met with Ribbentrop and made a deal with him. Berlin's plan for the military invasion of Poland was already completed, except the plan required use of the Slovakia road and railway system. Tiso, more than willing to comply with Hitler's wish, in return was to receive the cities of Pozsony, Nyitra, Eperjes, Zólyom, Besztercebánya, Selmecbánya and seventy villages. According to the 1920 census, the Slovak coveted area was inhabited by Hungarians, who made up more than fifty percent of the population.

The time table for the invasion of Poland was critical. The Tiso government obliged by establishing a government office for Slovak-German relations. Karmasin, a Gestapo agent, was appointed as department head of the new office. By July 23, an authoritarian, one-party political system was introduced in Slovakia. The constitutional charter considered the Slovak People's Party the only possessor of all rights and powers. Within three weeks, on August 18, the Slovak government signed the German-Slovak mutual aid agreement which gave form to the military structure of the country and placed the Slovak Army under the control of the German command. The German and Slovak armies, on August 19, advanced and reached the Slovak-Polish border. In less than two weeks, the German invasion of Poland began. Symbolically, the Slovak Government ordered general mobilization and without a formal declaration of war against Poland, the Slovak Army, under the control of the German command also invaded Poland.

It should have been no surprise to anyone on that March 15, 1939, that a people, having enjoyed the blessings of Austro-German culture for centuries, gave an enthusiastic welcome to Hitler's army, The Czechs felt comfortable within the framework of German protectorate. Many of them remembered their privileged positions under the Empire. They had German-Austrian education and spoke German well. The Czech heavy industry, as the Bruna factory assembling automobiles and airplanes or the Skoda-plants making cannons and tanks, switched over to German war production with no difficulty whatsoever. The Czech Fascist Party, named "Vlojka" (flag) and led by General Rudolf Gayda, played an important role in the swift and painless transition. The factory workers were eager to work overtime, for they received bonus ration cards and clothing coupons in return. The Czechs' capacity for self-accommodation was amazing. Servants of the absolutistic Rulers of Austria, they turned into advocates of Western Democracy during the First World War, posing as bulwark against the German "Drang nach Osten" and "the arrows of the barbarous Hungarians". When they felt that Western Democracy was in crisis, they embraced Nazism. And when Molotov and Ribbentrop signed the German-Russian Non-aggression Pact, in 1939, the Pan-Slav ambition of the Czechs flared up. This time they hoped to create a Great Slav Empire in Central Europe with the support of Germany and the cooperation of Soviet Russia. Their dream began to evaporate, when Hitler invaded Russia.

Masaryk's dream, however, was fulfilled in a fashion, when the Bolshevik armies of Russia swarmed all over the region, in the spring of 1945. And while the Soviet soldiers treated their Czech brethren well, for they did not touch the Czech women or the properties of Czech citizens, in Hungary, they raped thousands of women, plundered villages, sacked cities and grabbed and sent innumerable civilians to Siberia. Benes was quick to show gratitude by providing 20,000 ethnic Hungarians to the Soviet military. Under the direction of Jozef Lettrich, Istvan Kocvara and Miklos Ferjencik of the Slovak National Council, the unfortunate Hungarian slaves were used in the reconstruction of the Donec basin. [12]

CHAPTER 4

The Second Czechoslovak Republic
(1938-1948)

In October of 1938, due to mounting public pressure, Benes resigned and General Jan Syrovy was named as interim President of Czechoslovakia. Foreign Minister Krofta was replaced by Frantisek Chvalkovsky, formerly ambassador to Rome. On October 6, 1938, the State of Slovakia was proclaimed under the presidency of Josef Tiso.

Chvalkovsky was well connected among the diplomats of the Axis Powers. Syrovy, who was both interim President and Prime Minister of Czechoslovakia, was well known for his anti-Soviet stand. On the advice of Chvalkovsky, Syrovy dissolved the Communist Party and abrogated the non-aggression treaty with Russia. The Czechoslovak National Unity Party, "Narodui Snedjoceui", was founded in Prague, on November 16, 1938, and was immediately supported by the deputies of the Czech Fascist Party. The National assembly, on November 30, elected Emil Hacha as the third President of Czechoslovakia. In accordance with the Czechoslovak Constitution, Hacha was elected for a term of seven years. The new President called on Rudolf Berán, the leader of the Agrarian Party, to form the next government. The Slovakian Karol Sidor, was appointed as Deputy Prime Minister, Syrovy assumed the duties of Minister of Defence, and Chvalkovsky continued to hold the Foreign Affairs portfolio. As the Czechoslovak Government's orientation towards the Axis became obvious, the French Military Mission departed Prague in the December of 1938.

Early January of the following year, Hacha and Chvalkovsky met with Hitler, who demanded a complete turnabout in Czechoslovakia affairs. In an Attempt to counter the German influence, England and France gave sixteen million pounds to Czechoslovakia. This was to no avail, because on March 14, Czechoslovakia was split in two. Hacha placed Bohemia and Moravia under the protection of Germany.

However, he did not give up his presidency, and Hitler did not remove him from that post. Hacha therefore retained the title of President, even though he was politically powerless.

Benes, in the meantime, emigrated surprisingly not to Paris, where his old supporters were, but instead to London. Financially well off by now, Benes settled into a large hotel suite, provided himself with secretaries and attempted to settle in as the head of a state in exile. To his surprise, Benes received a cool welcome at the office of Prime Minister Chamberlain, who was engaged in compromise talks with Hitler. Benes, sensitive to political moods, carefully avoided mentioning Versailles, Trianon and the Little Entente and contented himself by praising the democracy of Czechoslovakia. With no visible British political support, Benes shifted his public activities and propaganda towards the United States. The Czech lawyers in London, in the meanwhile, decided that Benes was still President of the Republic, notwithstanding his resignation in 1938 and the fact that Hacha had been freely elected as President by the National Assembly in November, 1938. During his first year abroad, Benes did not call himself President, only as the head of a government in exile. When the National Council in exile was set up, it decided that the election of Hacha had been invalid. Reference was made to a "vis major", in justification of the decision. In short order, the Czechoslovak government-in-exile, was recognized by Great Britain, the Soviet Union and the United States. Now Benes enjoyed the privileged position of an exiled head of state. Posing in his restored dignity, he meted out medals to his compatriots in London, while the Czech and Slovak people prospered under German protectorate. Benes always spoke of Czechoslovakia, ignoring the self proclaimed independence of Slovakia from its dubious Czech partner. For the same reason, Hitler not trusting Czech loyalty, never raised a Czech army, instead relied on the Slovaks, who willingly took part in the invasion of Poland, leaving the Czechs to produce cannons and ammunition.

With the outbreak of the Second World War and the fall of the Chamberlain government, the climate changed in England. And so did the attitude toward Czechoslovakia and Benes. Winston Churchill was the new Prime Minister of Great Britain. Whereas Chamberlain did not recognize the Czechoslovak government-in-exile and had second thoughts on the Czech "democracy", Churchill single mindedly set out to unite the anti-German forces, and on July 23, Churchill formally recognized Benes and his government-in-exile. Seeing the growing international impotence of France and considering his relation with France as a burden, Benes "wrote off" the friendship of France, turning his back on the nation to whom he owed the creation of Czechoslovakia. In a study published in the "Foreign Affairs" journal, he denounced France as "corrupt, and rotten". And, when France collapsed in the summer of 1940, the British government treated the Czechoslovak emigres as allies and the British media, as if by the cue of a conductor, began to praise Czechoslovakia, as the "bastion" of European democracy.

While Churchill was embroiled in the diplomatic games of Teheran, Yalta and Potsdam, Benes, using his influence as head of the Czechoslovak government-in-exile, persuaded British politicians to encourage England to assume the role of a champion in the battle for Czechoslovakia's restoration. Although his diplomatic manoeuvring are not yet fully revealed, enough has surfaced to indicate that through Bene's influence, Anthony Eden, the Foreign Secretary in the Churchill government, in his reply during a question period in the House of Commons, said: "The British government no longer considers the Munich agreement binding. In determining the permanent frontiers of Czechoslovakia, our government will not be influenced by the changes of 1938."[13] With this success behind him, Benes was once again busy concocting plans and treaties. The next fruit of his work was the plan of a Polish-Czechoslovakia confederation. Benes presented it as the foundation of a new, peaceful Central Europe. He was prudently silent about the Soviet occupation of Eastern Poland and the age-old aversion of the Poles to the Russians. Being painfully aware of the Polish distrust of the Czechs, he avoided any discussion about the problems of Teschen at the Polish-Czech frontier. He knew equally well that England and Poland were tied by a mutual assistance pact and that Poland enjoyed American sympathy. Especially since Poland had engaged in a heroic fight against the aggressors, while Bohemia simply surrendered to the German forces. The Polish General, Sikorski was well connected politically in London and Washington. So the propaganda idea of confederation seemed to be useful... with or even without Polish consent. Benes, realizing that Hungary could not be completely ignored in the reconstruction of Central Europe, and making use of the friendship between Poland and Hungary, asked General Sikorski, the President of the Polish government-in-exile, to promote reconciliation between Czechoslovakia and Hungary for reasons of confederation. And, while the English politicians considered the idea of a Polish-Czech confederation a reasonable one, they felt that Hungary's joining the confederation should not be encouraged.

America had certain reservations about Benes and his cabinet-in-exile. There was formal diplomatic exchanges between Roosevelt and Benes, but nothing more. The influence in the United States of Milan Hodsa, who has openly turned away from a deceitful Benes, worried Benes greatly. Hodsa a self declared Slovak was staunchly accepted by the American Slovaks as their leader and representative. He did not allow his American followers to forget the Pittsburg Agreement, nor that Slovaks never received their autonomy or as much as equal status under the Benes-Masaryk Czechoslovak Regime. Roosevelt, although cautious, was not familiar enough with Czechoslovakian history and the Benes-Masaryk connection. And contrary to the isolationism of his predecessors, Franklin Roosevelt strongly favoured intervention in Europe. As an American, he believed that it was the duty of the United States as a world power, to maintain peace, especially since Europeans appeared incapable in resolving their differences. In his haste, Roosevelt sought the friendship of another world power, the Soviet Union, and unwittingly fell under the influence of Stalin. Further more, Roosevelt espousing to understand, in fact did not comprehend the intricate national problems of Europe. As a consequence to his misunderstanding, a divided Europe suffered under the Communist yoke for over forty-five years.

As his London government-in-exile did not enjoy the confidence of America, Benes wrote a lengthy article, in the 1942 New York periodical, "Foreign Affairs", on "The Organization of Post War

Europe". While the "Detruisez L'Autriche-Hongrie" was the 'bible' of the Czech propaganda campaign before the First World War, "The Organization of Post War Europe" contains Benes' blueprint for the reshaping of Central Europe after the Second World War. In the "Detruisez", Benes fought for the creation of Czechoslovakia, while in the "Organization", he lecturingly gave advice to the Great Powers on the new European order. He preached, that "Czechoslovakia must be liberated, or else there won't be peace in Europe... The foundation stone of the new Central Europe is to be the Polish-Czech confederation... Revision is out of the question. Hungary must be pushed back to its Trianon frontiers." Benes, like a good poker player, played his bluffs and there was not one Western politician or journalist, who would question or call his statements. There was no balancing article in the "Foreign affairs" pointing out that the Czech engineered Czechoslovakia was not created by a democratic process, was not run by democratic means, and certainly did not treat its minorities with democratic decency.

The Czech propaganda war was based on bluffs and on the general Western ignorance of European history and politics. The Benes government-in-exile had but one objective: the restoration of Benes' Czechoslovakia. It had to win over the American public opinion, because in 1942, England alone supported Benes. After the Teheran Conference of November 28, 1943, however, Benes saw a shift in the balance of power as far as Central Europe was concerned. While Roosevelt was enamoured by Stalin's Pan-Slav charisma, Churchill, unfortunately too late, understood the Soviet's intension and maintained an attitude of cool reserve during the conferences. Benes like Churchill understood, that the friendship between the Bolsheviks and the Western world would sooner or later come to an end, but not before Central Europe would fall into the Soviet sphere. With this realization, Benes called on his government-in-exile for an orientation change; a change toward the Soviet Union. Benes never hesitated to change sides or colours.

What the Allies would do in case of victory, in 1943 no one really knew. The English speaking nations did not publicize their plans for several reasons. First, because Stalin did not tell Churchill and Roosevelt what his plans were, or rather what he told them could hardly be believed. Secondly, they could not very well foresee the power relations at the end of the war. And finally, because there was a certain natural antagonism between Churchill and Stalin. As for Benes, he let the Allies know that Czechoslovakia expected to emerge as the leading, directive and executive power in Central Europe. His conception, which resembled Stalin's plans, did not exclude the further dismembered or, if need be, the virtual elimination of Hungary. In his New York published, "Organization of Post War Europe", Benes stated as much. He continuously referred to the humiliating and dismembering Treaty of Trianon as justification for his actions. He fiercely insisted that, "Hungary must not retain the territories awarded to it by Germany; for, breaking its treaties and   participation in a despicable war." Benes, however, was silent about the embarrassing fact, that the Czechs willingly served and prospered under Hitler, or that the Slovaks were willingly supported and joined the German Army in the invasion of Poland. Nor did he speak of the persistent cries of the Slovaks for self autonomy, which Hitler granted and lasted but a few years.

The London Czechoslovak government-in-exile had difficulties of its own. The Slovaks welcomed the estrangement of Hodsa and Benes. While Stefan Osusky, the wealthy American Slovak, turned away from the "Czechoslovak conception". Hodsa lashed out at the "Federation in Central Europe". He was for confederation but not 'Benes style'. Benes considered the October 6, 1938, 'Zsolna Decree', which granted self-government to Slovakia as meaningless. He never stopped scheming or uttering denouncements against anyone who did not agree with his ideas. And while he worked hard to assure the leading role for Czechoslovakia, he was never able to see fairly the needs of the neighbouring people. The feeling of solidarity was alien to him. Instead of seeking their friendship, he sought the favour of distant great powers, trying to gain distinction and privilege. His insistence on a Polish-Czech confederation was due to his awareness, that the Poles enjoyed better reputation in the West and Benes meant to use that in his own favour.

A hundred years earlier, the idea of confederation was introduced by Kossuth to the world. But Kossuth envisioned a peaceful co-operation of the Central European state, whereas Benes had the dominance of his beloved country in mind. There was a great difference between the two conceptions. Kossuth wrote,

> "We are surrounded by great powers, let us pool our resources and help one another, preserving our independence. Otherwise there won't be freedom and peace in Europe. Megalomania, ceaseless rivalry, old and new conspirations will characterize the life of nations. I am convinced that the confederation of the little nations along the Danube is imperative."[14]

Kossuth did not put one nationality above another. His confederation would have brought lasting peace in Central Europe. It is painfully clear that Benes could not comprehend this Danubian cooperative confederation, despite all his cleverness. To demonstrate, in the "Foreign Affairs" Benes wrote, "For Hungary, only one road would be open to prosperity, the possible joining to the Czechoslovak-Polish confederation. Otherwise, it would run into a second, more severe Trianon." Another example; Benes's answer to the minorities question was, "The population exchange must be facilitated and emigration encouraged", meaning that the large Hungarian minority living in Czechoslovakia, Rumania or Yugoslavia should be 'encouraged' to leave the land of their forefathers. Czech, Rumanian and Serbian settlers were to be provided as replacement for the displaced Hungarians. This was Benes' simple solution to the minority problem. And what would be the fate of those who did not want to emigrate? As it turned out, it was forced assimilation or oppression.

Benes once wrote that, "The protection of minorities should mean protection of democratic human rights and not protection of the rights of nations". Ignoring the protests of European minorities, between the two wars, against the misuse of the St. Germain Peace Treaty(September 10, 1919) clauses, which spoke of protection of minority rights for the use of one's own language and religion, and implying protection for inherent cultural rights, Benes argued for Czechoslovak national rights. Then, when it suited him, Benes blamed extreme nationalism for the outbreak of the second world war, saying that humanism was to be promoted rather than nationalism. Later, during the twenties and thirties, because it did not serve his purpose, Benes dismissed the true problem, which was not the nationalism of the minorities, but the chauvinism and imperialism of the majority. And while at Trianon, it served Benes to demand Czechs national rights, in Prague, Benes and his Czech government refused everything to their minorities, as the "Kassa Program" (Košicky Program) of 1945 clearly showed. Benes could in one moment wallow in his unbridled nationalism and in the next moment say: "Enough of Slovak nationalism, let us speak of democratic rights." His "protection of minorities" was a bluff, just like his "plans for confederation".

CHAPTER 5

Minority Reforms
(1944-1945)

The cool and reserve attitude of the English speaking powers left Benes dissatisfied, but the news from Moscow held out promises more to his liking. The Secretary General of the Czech Communist Party, Klement Gottwald, gained the support of his Russian comrades. Though Benes and Gottwald did not share the same political philosophy, the London based Czechoslovak government-in-exile believed the alignment of the two strategies was necessary to achieve their common objective. Benes flew to Moscow in December of 1943, for talks with Gottwald and Stalin. The Slav politicians found agreement in the radical resolution of Czechoslovakia's minority problems. They agreed that expatriation and driving out the Germans and Hungarians was the answer against future international accountability and reprisals. Benes was not the original author of such a plan. Tiso, the President of the Fascist Slovakia, and Mack, the partisan leader of the Hlinka Guards, planned to remove the Czechs and deport the Jews from Slovakia. In April of 1943, Tiso and Mack requested Hitler's approval to carry out the deportation, and then by using the Gypsies to fill the Slovak census count, they intended to do the same to the Hungarians. Once approval was received, they boldly announcement the Slovak agenda in the editorial of the Pozsony 'Gardista'.

In the Autumn of 1944, weeks before the Soviet Army reached the border of Slovakia, the Slovak National Council ordered the confiscation of Hungarian properties. The decree read,

"The land of our ancestors must return to the hands
of their Slovak descendants! Not one Hungarian
landowner will remain in Slovakia. Their properties
will be expropriated without any compensation" [15]

The Communist controlled Slovak National Council went further and declared, on February 4, 1945, that the new Czechoslovak Republic would be a popular democracy. It then summed up its policy towards the minorities in the following manner:

> "The new Republic guarantees the national rights of the Ukrainians. The partisans of magyarization (hungarianization) and the adherents of feudal system are enemies of the Slovak people. They have to leave our country. As for our citizens of Slovak origin, that are victims of forced magyarization, they may return to the life of our nation."

After the Second World War, with the introduction of the Czechoslovak 'minority reforms', began the Calvary for tens of thousands of Hungarian in Northern Hungary. Benes' radio statement, on February 16, 1945, made it very clear that his government intended to eradicate the Hungarian minority, in order to create a state of one nation and one language. In less than two weeks, on February 27, the Czechoslovak Government issued its Decree No. 4, ordering the confiscation of all Hungarian properties. The following explanation was given by Samuel Czambel to justify the government action:

> "The Hungarian and German minorities have always been strongholds of reactionism and fascism, irredentism and separatism in the time of the First Republic. This decree dispensed historical justice. The Slovak land, long in the hands of oppressors, was restored to Slovak hands."[16]

The 'Slovak land', which Czambel referred to, historically was Hungarian for over a thousand years. And, instead of presenting bonafide proof, as to how the Hungarians were their oppressors, Gustav Husak, during the next conference of the Slovak Communist Party declared that,

"In 1938, the great majority of Hungarians welcomed the mutilation of the Republic. The Magyars participated in the drive that sent our compatriots away from their homes.... We know that the whispering propaganda has not stopped. They believe this part of Slovak land will be returned to Hungary. They must understand, not a square kilometre will be returned to Hungary. We will not negotiate this question. The Slovak peasants and workers who were chased away will regain their ancient land."[17]

The fact, that the Northern Hungarian cities and towns of Csallóköz, Ipolyság, Kassa, Aranyosmarót, Rimaszombat and the county of Abaúj-Torna and others had no Slovak population before the Peace Treaty of Trianon did not bother Husak or his government.

The Slovak Communist Party continued its minority persecutions. On March 1, 1945, it published its Kassa Manifesto. After the usual preamble, the decree went on to justify the Government's action which was a direct result of, as they put it,

"...the Hungarian crimes committed against the Slovak nation. ...Therefore, the Slovak Communist Party feels justified in giving orders as follows:
--All Hungarians living in the territory of Slovakia who assisted in, or welcomed, the occupation of the Southern portion of Slovakia, and all those who mistreated a Slovak citizen, will be summoned to court. These are to be convicted and punished as the enemies of democracy and of the Slovak nation.
--The Slovak Communist Party solemnly announces its plan for the systematic assimilation of Hungarians living in the areas where the Slovak population had been forcefully magyarized.
--Slovakia is indivisible."[18]

The above manifesto was written by the Party whose Secretary-General in 1945, became the President of the Republic forty years later. Gustav Husak.

These preliminary events led to the promulgation of the 'Kassa Program", which was the source of unprecedented oppression for the Hungarian minority in Czechoslovakia. Deprivation of their civil rights, inhuman humiliation, ruthless deportations were the fate of a great many unfortunate Hungarians during those three long years.

CHAPTER 6

The Kassa Program
(1945-1948)

The rapid unfolding of events starting with the Manifesto and ending with the Kassa Program proclamation was remarkable. On May 5, 1945, President Benes, to underscore the Kassa Program, declared in a radio broadcast, that "This state belongs to the Czechs and Slovaks, no one else!". Within weeks, Hungarians living in Czechoslovakia lost their citizenship, with the exception of those, who had participated in the resistance and those who had been persecuted for their loyalty to the Republic. The Kassa Program reduced 98% of the Hungarian population in Northern Hungary's Czechoslovakia to homelessness. The first visible manifestation of the program was in the Slovak National Council Decree No.45, which ordered the immediate dismissal of all Hungarians working as civil servants. Decree No.69 directed private companies to dismiss their Hungarian employees. After this, all Hungarian schools, cultural, social and sport associations were closed. A Hungarian author and journalist in Czechoslovakia, Zoltán Fábry, recorded that in the Autumn of 1945, posters appeared on the walls in Kassa, with the following inscription:

"If you wish to see a barbarian, look at a Hungarian !"[19]

The Czechoslovak Government strategy for the implementation of their Hungarian Minority Program, otherwise known as the Kassa Program, was designed over four progressively escalating phases:

1. Expulsion,
2. Population exchange,
3. Forced assimilation and
4. Deportation.

1. Expulsion receiving top priority was implemented immediately after the proclamation of the Kassa Program. Some 30,000 Hungarian

intellectuals were accused of being war criminals, without trial or legal recourse, and were ordered to leave the country.

2. Population exchange appeared the next and easiest phase, because the Czechoslovak Government believed that the Potsdam Conference would provide the mandate for their program. To ensure international approval, the Czechoslovakian cabinet dispatched a memorandum to the Potsdam Conference, (which was sitting between July 17 and August 2, 1945) in which their government contended, that the Great Powers must order the immediate removal of all Hungarians from Czechoslovakia for the sake of lasting peace in Central Europe. Roosevelt now dead, Truman represented the United States, Attlee Great Britain, and of course, Stalin spoke for the Soviet Union. The main items on the conference agenda were: reparations, territorial adjustments and the question of free elections. Mass expatriation of a minority was as yet unprecedented in the history of European political sanctions. The Potsdam Conference, although consenting to the expatriation of the Sudeten Germans back to Germany, saw most members strongly objected to the removal of Hungarians from Czechoslovakia. Supported only by the Soviet delegates, the Czechoslovak demand failed to materialize. This meant, that without international support to realize their population exchange plans, Czechoslovakia had to negotiate directly with Hungary.[20]

The Czechoslovak Government, in exasperation issued its Decree No.33, on August 2, 1945, the day the Paris Conference closed. The decree meant to punish Hungarians on the grounds of "collective responsibility". This decree became the foundation for all future decrees, which were to deprive nearly a million people of all their social, economic, political and cultural rights. Kálmán Janics pointed out, that decrees No.33 and No.108 went as far as the punitive laws of the Fascist Slovakia, in 1942, when the Jews of the area lost their citizenship and personal properties. The anti minority feelings became fashionable once again, as a result of the Potsdam fiasco. In the Czechoslovak cities, individuals speaking Hungarian were often insulted and the Hlinka Guardsmen provoked bloody fights in predominantly Hungarian villages. At the Democratic Party Congress, in October 1945, the party leader, Lettrich, in an emotional outburst spluttered, that "We cannot tolerate the members of a nation that has undermined our state! Let them go where their hearts draw them." [21] Juraj Zvara, a Slovak historian, recorded the following observations about the forced population exchange of 1945:

> "In Hungary, 95,421 Slovaks responded to the call for resettlement. The number of those who actually moved to Slovakia was 73,273 for over 22,000 had changed their minds. The resettlers left 31,308 cadastral acres behind. In Slovakia, the authorities designated 105,047 Hungarians for the exchange. In fact, 68,407 were transported south and 6,000 or so voluntarily, 74,407 altogether. They left 109,295 cadastral acres behind." [22]

The assumption in Prague was, that some half a million Slovaks were living in Hungary, 400,000 or so were expected to take part in the exchange. They figured if that many Slovaks were transferred, the problem with the Hungarian minority would disappear. As it turned out, less than 100,000 Slovaks lived south of the border in Hungary and 22,000 of those preferred to stay. This caused surprise, disappointment and embarrassment in Prague. To lessen their chagrin, Czechoslovakia at the September 1946 Paris Peace Conference proposed the expatriation of 200,000 more Hungarians. This proposal, once again, was only supported by the Soviets delegates, and once again international approval was not given. Instead, in their favour, Czechoslovakia was granted a minor territorial adjustment and told to solve their minority problems through direct negotiations with the other countries involved. After the flat denial at the Paris Conference, Czechoslovakia did not wish to discuss the population exchange program with Hungary.

3.   Forceful assimilation was the next to last phase of a persistent drive in the Czechoslovak minority program. On June 17, 1946, Prague government issued yet another decree, in which it offered two alternatives to the remaining 400,000 Hungarians still living in

Slovakia. "Whoever professed to become a Slovak, can regain his or her citizenship, however, whoever does not, will be persecuted." The Czechoslovakian essayist, Garantier, in his study, "Reslovakizacia a jej zdovodnenie" (In defence of re-Slavonization), blatantly justified this policy in the following manner: "...In this way we wish to recover what used to be ours."[23] He was only mirroring the words of a departmental order (20,000/1946) published on June 17, which read,

> "The forcefully Magyarized Slovaks will not be expatriated. These are victims of the chauvinist policy of the old Hungary. They will be given the chance to return to their own."

The Czechoslovak Government or its advocates were unable to provide any credible proof, that there has ever been in Greater of Lesser Hungary any 'Magyarization' of Slovaks. There is however, ample proof of Slavonized Hungarians living in the democratic Republic of Czechoslovakia. For the many Hungarians, living in their Northern Hungary, which was now Czechoslovakia, the government order created a terrible dilemma. Their bread, their life, their very existence was at stake. Between of June 17 and July 1, 1946, 410,820 Hungarians had to deny their nationality, culture and mother tongue, in order to survive. Most of the applications were written with shaking hands. Out of those, 84,141 applications were rejected and their applicants were declared "Persona non grata", in other words outlaws. The figures of the 1950 Czechoslovak census reflected the pressures suffered by the Hungarian minority. The census found, that in Slovakia now only 367,733 proclaimed their Hungarian ancestry.

4.   Deportation! As if all that passed before was not enough. The expulsions, the population exchange and the psychological terror did not result in what the Czechoslovak Government wanted to accomplish. It had decided to liquidate the "foreign body" in its state. Because the Paris Conference rejected the idea of mass expatriation, the Czechoslovak government resorted to its ultimate plan, the mass deportation of Hungarians to scatter settlements in the depopulated Sudetenland. This was what Stalin had ordered for the undesirable

ethnic minorities of Russia. Stalin was quoted as having said, that the solution to the 'Hungarian problem' was only a question of railway cars. Taking a cue from Stalin, Vladimir Clementis, Deputy Foreign Minister, in his October 31, 1946, address to the Czechoslovak National Assembly did not mince words when he said,

> "The Hungarians must be moved to the Sudetenland
> by force. ...We have a right to assimilate the
> Magyars and create a state of one nation, even by the
> way of dispersion of the unwilling."[24]

His statement was quoted by the 'Narodna Obroda', the official publication of the Slovak National Council, in its November 13, 1946 issue. Another Slovak paper, the 'Pravda', put it this way,

> "Our government, if it cannot reach an agreement
> with Hungary, will find a way to solve the problem
> created by the Hungarian ethnic group in our
> country, after all it is our home affair. In any case,
> Slovakia will not be tainted with other
> nationalities."[25]

The forced deportation, which started on November 19, 1946, and lasted most of the Winter, finally ended on February 25, 1947. Reports on the operations filled the Slovak papers for many days. The paper 'Slovensky Vychod' announced,

> "We will employ Hungarians in Czech areas. We
> will set things right, if Czechoslovakia and Hungary
> cannot come to an agreement and the exchange of
> population cannot be put into effect."

The deportations were controlled by the Slovak army and police. Military units surrounded the villages, one after the other, and ordered all the families to pack up without delay. They were allowed to take their most important personal belongings, and nothing else. Their property was expropriated and confiscated. The account of Zvara Juraj provides statistical data on the deportations: the drive affected 9,610 families, 41,640 individuals. The victims were moved from 393 villages, 17 districts. Among the deported were 5,128 small landowner families. The number of casualties caused by violence and severe cold (transportation was provided via unheated cattle-trucks) amounted to nearly 1,000. The removed Hungarian landowners were replaced by Slovak settlers from the mountainous regions of Slovakia, or Czech peasants. There was no compensation or indemnity whatsoever.

Zoltán Fábry's memoirs written in May of 1946, 'The accused speaks out', in the author's own words, was like a "scream in a vacuum". The memoir documented the shameful, inhuman treatment of the Hungarian minority, and in turn demanded justice. His memoir, which was addressed it to all the leading Slovak and Czech intellectuals and politicians drew no response. He recalled this years later, as he wrote,

> "When the accused spoke up in 1946, no audience was granted him. My S.O.S. was ignored. The 80 page letter, sent to all leading politicians and many members of the Czechoslovak intelligentsia, translated into their own language, elicited no reply. This general indifference, this callous insensibility was terrible!!"

János Gyöngyösi, the Foreign Minister of Hungary, during the August 14, 1946 Paris Peace Conference protested the plight of the Hungarian minorities in Czechoslovakia, and was able to table discussions on their behalf. Jan Masarky, the Foreign Minister of Czechoslovakia in his fabricated reply the following day sighted that the leaders of the Hungarian minority were in league with the bloody Lidice Frank movement and demanded sanction for the immediate deportation of all Hungarians from Czechoslovakia. Knowing that both the United States and the United Kingdom had declared this "solution" unacceptable, Masaryk continued by saying, that "The deportation of the Hungarians was inevitable!". While the Soviet Union accepted and supported the Masaryk fabrication, the Western Powers becoming aware of the appalling record of Slovak fascism, ordered the deportations to cease. Shockingly, on February 10, 1947, at the conclusion of the Peace Conference, the ensuing Treaty did not contain any clauses, which would have provided some guarantee of minority rights for the three million Hungarians living in Czechoslovakia, Yugoslavia and Romania.

The peace negotiations were still going on when Zoltán Fábry demanded justice and asked questions, such as,

> "Why do the victors trample upon the Hungarian ethnic group whose writers and leaders gave proof of their honesty and fairness between the two world wars? Why did the Slovakian Hungarian leader, János Esterházy, alone have the courage to try to stem the tide called national socialism?"

János Esterházy, was the head of the United Hungarian Party, and a member of the Slovak National Assembly, in 1944. His was the only dissenting voice who opposed the Fascists and the Slovak Parliamentary Bill, 68/1942, which ordered the deportation of Jews from Slovakia. Soon after, on October 15, 1944, he was imprisoned by the Nazis, because he refused to reform his party to the specifications of Nazi ideology. After the occupation of Slovakia by the Soviet troops, by the request of the new Slovak government, he was declared a war-criminal, and was deported to Russia. On September 18, 1947, in Pozsony (Bratislava), the Slovak Socialist Government, in absentia, sentenced Esterházy to death. His death sentence was later reduced to life imprisonment due to international intervention and for lack of evidence. Esterházy died in a Soviet prison hospital.

CHAPTER 7

Twenty Years Later
(1964)

The Hungarian minority had to wait twenty years for an answer to Fabry's questions. Juraj Zvara, the Czechoslovakian historian and 'apologist', in the 1964 issue #5 of the 'Prehled', published two studies on the events between 1945 and 1948. He acknowledged, that there were injustices perpetrated against the Hungarian minority. Attempting to place it in a "historical perspective", he argued that the decrees that deprived the Hungarians of their rights were elicited by the internal situation and external causes. He then proceeded to describe those external causes.

> "It must be understood, that the international situation held the very real possibility and threat of a Western Imperialists invasion of our Republic, which was fuelled by the Czechoslovak and Hungarian bourgeoisie living in Hungary, exploiting the unsolved minority problems within our borders. This uncertainty, the fear of invasion compelled the Czechoslovak Communist party to proclaim the Kassa Decrees, designed to forestall the repetition of the Munich or Vienna decisions. This was the reason for the negotiations with Hungary in 1945 and 1946, in regard to an exchange of population. This is why we demanded in Paris the approval of the population exchange or if necessary, of the removal of the Magyars from Czechoslovakia. In order to eliminate the cause of ceaseless arguments, which would certainly be an impediment to consolidation. For this reason, the Paris peace conference recognized Czechoslovakia as the state of the Czech and Slovak nations."[26]

Zvara conveyed the opinion, that the outside invasion was expected to come from Hungary. Since, by 1947, the fear of invasion had sufficiently dissipated, in Zvara's words, that "the gradual restoration of rights was allowed to take place." The internal causes, Zvara blamed on Benes, the President of Czechoslovakia. Zrava supported the notion that the pre-communist regime, meaning Benes, singularly and with premeditation planned the disposal of the non-Slav minorities in Czechoslovakia. To prove the point, he quoted Benes saying, "I predicted in November 1938 that the inevitable war would be hardest on the minorities.", He continued to quote from a message sent by Benes, on October 28, 1945, to the provisional National Assembly, "Those members of the national minorities who refuse to return to their own country, will have to submit to the process of assimilation.

Zvara's attempts to justify the post war Czechoslovak actions were poor, to say the least. His references, to the danger of an impending invasion, had no merit. The Hungary of 1945, writhing in economic and political ruin, militarily paralyzed and occupied by the Russians, was incapable of invading Czechoslovakia. Further more, his translucent argument, unworthy of a historian, tried to make the demand of the Czechoslovak delegation at the Paris Conference appear positive, " In order to eliminate the cause of ceaseless arguments, which would certainly be an impediment to consolidation.". His singular accusation of Benes and the Slovak Democratic Party for being responsible for the injustices, completely scorns the significant role the Communist Party played in the persecution of the minorities. Equally, he kept silent about the Benes-Gottwald agreement of 1943, concerning the solution of the minority problems. Zvara blatantly avoided the mention of the February 1945 proclamation of the Slovak National Assembly or the March 1, 1945, Manifesto of the Slovak Communist Party, which severally curtailed the civil rights of the Hungarians. Indeed, the Communist Party played a greater role in the contrivance of the Kassa Program, than the bourgeois parties or Benes himself.

An International Code of Law for the protection of political, cultural, religious, economic and linguistic rights of national minorities must be assured by international guarantees. Should a government violate those rights, the victims of injustice and persecution should be able to appeal to an International Forum. The now past communist states did not recognize international guarantees nor the need for an international forum. Moreover, they saw the minority problems as an internal affair and cared little, in the way of written protection, for the rights of their minority. During the year of the 'Prague Spring' of 1968, the Hungarian Authors' Association of Slovakia articulated its cultural claims, without trespassing on the question of loyalty to the State of Czechoslovak. In the journal of the "Kulturny Zivot", Rudolf Olsinsky reacted by comparing the "demands" of the Hungarian writers to those of the West German revanchist. Daniel Okáli, the head of the expatriation committee from 1946 to 1948, pointedly observed, that the Kassa Program can be easily reactivated in 1968, since to date, it has not been rescinded.

With the suppression of the 'Prague Spring', the Soviet Union once again forcefully asserted its will on the internal affairs of Czechoslovakia and helped the anti-Hungarian drive to flare up once again. The Soviet tanks crushed not only Dubchek, but the Hungarian minority's aspirations. The life and fate of the Hungarians in Slovakia after 1968, provided little hope for optimism. Minority rights, discriminatory cultural and religious practices, suppressive school policies, economic and social depravations continued to be the order of the day for the minorities.

Perfunctorily, the Czechoslovak government introduced certain minority guarantees into its October 1968 Constitution. However, the few elementary rights of minorities, supposedly guaranteed by the new constitution, did not address the social and economic inequality of the Slav and non-Slavs of the country. The legislative exercise was for foreign consumption. Domestically, even those small guarantees and programs, allowing for the schooling of the minorities in their own language, freedom for minorities to participate in cultural gatherings and clubs, and provision for government services in minority languages, were never formally promulgated to the country's thousands of civil servants, which would have ensured the enactment and enforcement of the new constitutional edicts, specifically pertaining to the minorities. The racist and undemocratic spirit of the Kassa Program, continued to find a strong voice in the new Czechoslovak Constitution. Constitutional articles 1960/100, 1968/143 and 1968/44 pointedly distinguished between the natural people of the state (ie. the Czech and the Slovaks) and the other national minorities. This was and still is a violation of the international agreement, which disallowed the enactment of racially or ethnically discriminatory legislation, and was signed by all members of the Potsdam Conference, including Czechoslovakia,

The economic policy of the Czechoslovak state and especially that of the Slovak Socialist Republic since 1968 continued to maintain its discriminatory attitude. The one thousand square kilometre area in Southern Slovakia, populated by Hungarians, became and still is, one of the most neglected areas. The government refused aid and development to the population. This meant, that part of the population became doomed into idleness. Ignoring international agreements on economic, social and cultural rights, which imposes certain obligations on the participating states to guarantee the right to work for every individual, Czechoslovakia by neglect encouraged deliberately the plunging of this area into backwardness. This, predominantly Hungarian populated, area was economically and socially suppressed to become the poorest, with the lowest average income per capita in Czechoslovakia. Job openings became few. Nearly 40% of the working portion were forced to leave the area, temporarily or for good, and look for jobs elsewhere. Only 30% of the women who were able and willing to work could find a job. And yet, the government grants, then as now, are scarce and extremely low, about 25% of what other parts of Slovakia receive.

The Czechoslovakian educational policy towards its minorities, after 1968 to the present, remained harsh and unyielding. The educational policy of the Slovak Socialist Republic was aimed at the elimination of all Hungarian schools and of the Hungarian language. The authorities disregarding parental wishes, use all means of persuasion to ensure that Hungarian parents send their children to Slovak schools. This hinderance in cultural and academic progress caused great psychological problems to many. The situation in the nurseries and kindergartens was deplorable. The government's attitude towards its minorities, selectively ignored its own 1959 declaration, in which, edict #2 outlined the principle, that "the child enjoys special protection and must be given the opportunity to develop and grow, physically, mentally, morally and socially, in freedom and dignity." The disadvantages of Hungarian children increased as they reached higher levels of education. Inevitably it led to the present economic backwardness. The number of unskilled labourers in this area is staggering.

In his book, "In a common fatherland...", published in 1972, Juraj Zvara, criticized the lower-grade authorities for sabotaging the constitutional law. He wrote:

> "Bilingualism should have won acceptance in public
> places, in verbal communication with clients, in
> official letters and publications, in the courts. Public
> building, stores institutes should have bilingual names
> and villages, towns as well... The statutes have
> never been fully observed."

This criticism should have come twelve years earlier. For, in the 1960's, pure Hungarian communities were transformed into mixed ones. The administration was completely reorganized in South-Slovakia. The re-Slavonised clerks, were moved to Slovak districts, while Slovaks who did not speak Hungarian were moved to the new mixed communities. Before 1960, there were seven districts with distinct Hungarian majority. After 1960, there was only one! Zvada continued his account:

> "The minority problems were more and more
> neglected. There were interferences in their
> educational affairs and disregard of the principle of
> bilingualism. In 1961 Hungarian schools were
> changed into Slovak-Hungarian ones. In many

schools, teaching in Hungarian was discontinued. These drastic changes brought about resistance and protests. "

Between 1950 and 1975, 223 Hungarian public schools were forced to close and Hungarian children were compelled to learn in an alien language. The orders of the Minister of Education in the Slovak Socialist Republic determined the percentage of Hungarian pupils to be taught in Slovak schools. As an example, in the Dunaszerdahely district, where 80% of the population are Hungarian, schooling in Hungarian, in 1983, was only available to 40% of the children. In 1978, by ministerial decree, 15% fewer Hungarians than Slovaks were authorized to attend high schools, and in the trade schools the imbalance was 39%. These regulations applied to all high schools, regardless of the language used. Progressively the proportional disparity has become worse and not better since 1978. The 1978 educational proclamation allowed for one and only one Hungarian highschool in a Hungarian district, regardless of the number of applicants. The use of Hungarian, in the authorized minority trade schools with mixed student population, was discouraged gradually, through reduced government funding. Since 1977, through financial and social restrictions, fewer and fewer Hungarian teachers were given college training opportunities.

Politically, culturally, economically and socially defenceless, the Hungarian minority had only one government approved legal association in Czechoslovakia, the 'CSEMADOK'. This purely 'Cultural Association', was under the strict control of the Slovak Socialist Republic's Ministry of Cultural Relations. In 1972, the association was ejected from the National Front, because of its open opposition to the government and its mistreatment of minorities.[27] With little international recognition or aid, the cause of the Hungarian minority received a short world wide notice, through the work of one man. He single handedly stopped the Czechoslovak governmental machinery and made it retreat, if only for a little while. His name was Miklós Duray.

CHAPTER 8

The Fate of Duray
and the Kassa Program

The case of Duray received world attention in the nineteen-eighties. In 1978, Duray, author and geologist, founded the Committee for the Protection of Hungarian Minority Rights in Czechoslovakia. He firmly believed, that organized resistance to oppression could do more than scattered protests. His committee managed to foil the first renewed attempt on the part of the Czechoslovak Government to close down the Hungarian schools still in operation.

The Committee founded by Duray took up the fight against the constant pressure to make Hungarian education impossible in Slovakia. Government manipulation forced the public schools from grades five and higher to teach classes only in Slovak. There were some exceptions, such as Hungarian geography and history. The training of Hungarian teachers was curtailed by funding restrictions. When Hungarian and Slovak schools were combined, all subjects were taught in Slovak, regardless of the fact, that Hungarian pupils attending were in majority. Hungarian language education was further restricted to two or three hours per week. When confidential departmental documents, outlining the covert government intent to gradually eliminate Hungarian education format from the school system, were leaked to the public by the Duray Committee. Shortly after the disclosure, Government reprisal came swiftly, and Duray found himself under arrest and charged with agitating national minorities.

His organization spread the news of the blatant governmental discrimination and suppression far and wide, especially beyond the border of Czechoslovakia. Observers from many countries attended his trial. His brave self-defense and his thorough knowledge of the laws, coupled with the pressure of world opinion, once again made the Czechoslovak authorities retreat. The unexpected resistance forced the government into retreat. The trial proceeding were adjourned and Duray was allowed to go free, for the time. During the trial preliminaries, it became obvious to the international observers, as well as the rest of the world, that the Slovak nationalists in power, supported by their late Soviet patrons, would not give up their original intention in making Czechoslovakia a state for only Czechs and Slovaks.

On November 25, 1983, the Czechoslovak Government adopted a bill, which read,

> "the Ministry of Education may permit, that in a school belonging to an ethnic group certain subjects be taught in Czech or Slovak, if the national Committee of that district, in unison with the parents of Slovak or Czech pupils, applies for it; the same ministry may order, that certain subjects be taught in a language other than the 'teaching language' of the school."

Once again, the bill was aimed at the liquidation of the Hungarian school system. It was also in direct contravention of the constitutional law, which was passed on October 27, 1968, and was to guarantee the rights of national minorities to education in their own language, and concluded with the statement, that "all forms of denationalization are prohibited". The passing of the bill elicited loud protests in the Hungarian communities in South Slovakia. Ten-thousand Hungarians protested in letters against the ministerial order. Duray personally appealed to Gustav Husak, the President of the Republic, against the unconstitutionality of the bill. The Duray Committee organized several large protest rallies. As part of their protest, Duray's book entitled "Kutyaszorito" (Cornered) was published by Püski Publishers in New York. The foreword by Sándor Csoóri, stripped the self-contradiction of socialist internationalism to the buff, while the book graphically depicted the harrowing details of life in the stifling atmosphere of chauvinism. The bill was revoked. However, Juraj Busa, the Minister of Education, said at a press conference that the intent of the bill would reappear some other way.

The frankness of the book won Duray his second arrest, this time the government intended to isolated him from the world. Even his wife was not allowed to see him. In a series of delaying tactics, the trial was repeatedly put off, even though the indictment was prepared and submitted to the courts. After a lengthy prison term, Duray was finally charged for, "...sullying the name and reputation of the Republic". The New York based 'Hungarian Human Rights Foundation' expressed its outrage and demanded the immediate release of Duray, and that the Czechoslovak Government exercise basic respect for the human rights of the Hungarian minority in Slovakia.

The Czechoslovak political climate began to change in the mid nineteen-eighties. The advocates of arbitrary rule were replaced by new, younger and more sober men. Before the demise of the Czechoslovak Communist Regime, there were courageous critics of the system, like Jan Cernogursky, a Pozsony lawyer, and Milan Simecka, Prague philosopher, who condemned, in their open letters, the harassment of Duray. They laid bare the guilt of the Slovak socialist-nationalists and denounced their chauvinistic ways. The unexpected opposition by their own, bewildered the people in high power. In their confusion they resorted to means that turned the world opinion once more against them. But the Duray event passed and the injustices it tried to oppose and bring to the attention of the world became overshadowed by greater events.

And though, the ideology may have changed once again in Czechoslovakia, the national self importance and collective fear due to past and present trespasses still remain. The Hungarian past, in Northern Hungary, is being systematically erased. In Southern Slovakia, thousand year old settlements, villages, towns have been renamed. Usage of the old names in the media is prohibited. Not long ago, the printing of city names in their old Hungarian forms, such as Pozsony or Kassa (ancient cities of Hungary), in newspapers or magazines, was punishable by fines of 20,000 Coronas. In ancient Hungarian cities, which as a result of Trianon, are now part of Czechoslovakia, and where Hungarians are still in the majority, the old Hungarian street names were changed to reflect the rule of the new national majority. Even in the city of Komárom, the street named after one of Hungary's greatest writers, Mór Jókai, was marred by Slavonification, when local authorities translated his name into Slovak ("Jokaiho ulica"). In today's Hungary, where the voluntary Slovak settlers have preserved their own language for centuries, bilingual street signed attest to their welcomed presence in the community. While in Czechoslovakia, Hungarians are held in the bondage of contempt, discrimination, poverty, suffering and homelessness.

CHAPTER 9

Autonomy or Confederation
for the Twenty-first Century

In the early eighty's a Slovak World Congress was convened, specifically to gather all Slav and neighbouring groups outside Czechoslovakia, for a general 'scientific conference'. Western European and North American emigre Pole, Austrian, Czech, Slovak and Hungarian professionals from all disciplines were invited to the conference. For the first three days, the meetings held a scientific aura, but over the remaining sessions the debates turned political and secretive.

The most significant feature of the first half of the conference was the collective recognition that the future of Europe depended, to a great extent, on the sensible solution to the burning problems created by the peace treaties. At the time of the conference, Europe was more clearly divided. It was controlled by two spheres of interest. As a result of the artificial division, a fatal consequences was realized by all conference participants. The Danubian Basin had become politically, economically and financially a weightless region, incapable of defending, supporting and financing itself. Ultimately, the region was reduced to the role of a pawn in the rivalry and political gamesmanship of the Great Powers.

United Europe, the central theme of the Congress, was abandoned as soon as members fully realized that the problems of Europe, which started with the events leading up to and culminating at Trianon of 1920 required a confederation type of a solution. And as the Slovaks themselves felt more the victims than beneficiaries of the Czecho-Slovak confederacy, the antagonism between the Slovaks and the Czechs deepened during the debates. The Slovak stand did not leave any room for compromises: "They wanted neither Hungarian, nor Czech confederation!" The Slovak need for an independent, autonomous Slovakia was a major blow to the idea of Central European bonding. No sooner had the topic been introduced, the great Danubian Confederation debate ended on a disinterested note. Participants felt that further discussion was a waste of time.

The second part of the conference was more exclusive, echoing tunes of earlier Pan-Slav Congresses. The pro-Soviet Czech and Ruthenian delegation introduced the Pan-Slav debate by promoting the idea of a Pan-Slav Empire. Only the Serbians liked the idea, however they saw the geographic position of Hungary as an obstacle. Against this, the voices of independence were raised by the ABN (Anti-Bolshevik Block of Nations). Ukrainian representatives had their minds set on an independent Ukraine, which would absorb the Ruthenians and Slovaks of Northern Hungary, should they be willing to join. The Croatians and Macedonians also insisted on autonomy and self-government. And all the while, the Slovak delegates loudly called for independence to the great chagrin of Czechs.

In the heat of the argument an emigre Czech representative stood up and unfolded a map. He declared, to the astonishment of all, that the annexation of Czechoslovakia by the Soviet Union was imminent - the Moscow time table was geared for a 1984-1986 absorption. Authored by the chairman of the Czechoslovak Federal Council, Dr. Jiri Kotas, a memorandum, detailing the Soviet plan, and calling for resistance, was circulated to Western governments at the time. According to Dr. Kotas, Crozier, Brian, Elliott and other political analysts had known about the Soviet plan since 1976, when Brezhnev announced it at the Communist Party Congress. Brezhnev stated that a common frontier between Poland and Hungary could not be allowed to exist. The annexation of Czechoslovakia was to bring Eastern Germany into the immediate vicinity of the Soviets.

In fact, the softening process began in the Communist paper, "Mlada Fronta", with the article of professor Dzunusov, a Soviet philosopher. The article spoke of a new society with close political and economic ties and unity of purpose. The Freedom Communicating International News Agency, based on, Josef Josten, its Moscow correspondent's report, described the Soviet "Master Plan" for the absorption of the surrounding socialist states. In his report Josten pointed to the fact, that in 1977 Soviet Constitution was amended to include the statement, that "A socialist state wishing to join the Republic will not be refused".

The Czechoslovak Communist Party in 1978 received specific instructions for the psychological preparation of the masses. The rationalization behind and the conditions of the "voluntary joining" were outlined in the following points:

1. In Czechoslovakia little resistance is expected since the Marxist-Socialist idealogy has many old and faithful supporters there.

2. The Czechoslovak economy and the economy of the Soviet Union must stand on he same basis. In order to realize this, a new 5 year plan must be made on the Soviet pattern.

3. A system of civil rights that corresponds to the Soviet system, must be introduced.

4. The Czechoslovak military force is to be reorganized on the Soviet pattern. And every Czechoslovak army officer must learn the Russian language.

5. Wide-gauge rail-roads should be constructed between the two countries. And new highways.

6. Uniform currency must be introduced. The official language should be Russian.

7. The Soviet Education must be the model. The Czechoslovak Academy of Sciences must become affiliated to the Moscow Academy of Sciences.

8. Political conflicts must be judged and resolved through the Soviet system of legislation.

The Soviet Government hoped that all these conditions would be fulfilled by 1984-86. The occupation of Czechoslovakia was to be done with the help of the East-German army. Prior to this, the unreliable Czech Police Department was to be dissolved. Hungary was to be considered a buffer state. If needed, a combined Czechoslovak-Russian army was to be used against a rebellious Hungary. The disclosure caused great excitement and over shadowed the Pan-Slav dream and the conference.

Since that Slovak World Congress, new events have drastically changed the political landscape of Central and Eastern Europe and the balance of world power. And while the Soviet Empire is but a bad memory, in its denouement it left a legacy of ethnic discontent, jealousy and hatred. In Central and Eastern Europe, one by one, the small communist states peacefully or otherwise are attempting to turn the tide in favour of democracy. States, forged by the misguided will of ambitious politicians, are now attempting to disassociate themselves into their pre 20th Century dream of culturally independent and autonomous states. And, for history not to repeat itself again, it would be wise, for once, to learn from past mistakes and listen to the needs of people. For the Great Powers, this is not the time to engage in theoretical gamesmanship, especially in the light of the present world situation. A situation full of mistrust, conflict and economic hardship. Instead, this is the time of firm support and recognition of states crying for independence.

History has vividly shown, that forceful cultural unification, assimilation, relocation, or dispersal only breeds generations of hatred and conflict. Because it is difficult to change old grudges into goodwill and cooperation overnight, all political leaders must look to short term practical solutions with which all combatants can identify. Therefore, any attempt at federation, at this time, would be inflammatory. International healing can only be achieved, if national groups are allowed to form autonomous independent states of their own. Political stability within a state follows after external irritants are removed. Once the basic needs of self determination are met, the need for economic survival will follow, which causes a state to provide work and goods for its people. With small countries, the need to share and exchange is inevitable, and soon a dialogue will develop between states leading to commerce, trade and mutual sharing of natural resources. Once this period of healing and natural growth has taken place the need for mutual protection and economic survival will open the required dialogue amongst the Danubian states to forge a mutual aid or federative plan.

The lessons of the past set the premise for the outcome of the future. Today, the pre-Trianon borders cannot be re-established. But holding a plebescite in the succeeding states, to allow people a choice in deciding what country or state they want to be part of is a fundamental need and a must for international peace and Central European unity.

FOOTNOTES:

(PART III.)

1. Kettős Járom Alatt A Csehszlovákiai Magyarok Nemzeti Bizottmányának jelentés, 1951 (The Czechoslovak Hungarian Minority Commission Report, 1951), Published in Twinsburg, Ohio, March issue 1985.

2. Borsody, István Magyarok Csehszlovákiában. Az Ország Utja. (Hungarians in Czechoslovakia. The way of the country.), June 1938.

3. Sulyok, Dezső Magyar tragédia I. (Hungarian Tragedy vol. I.) Newark, 1954, pg 163.

4. Borsody, István Magyarok Csehszlovákiában. Az Ország Utja. (Hungarians in Czechoslovakia. The way of the country.), June 1938.

5. Kovács, Imre Magyarország megszállása (Hungary's occupation), Toronto, Vörösváry, 1979, pg376.

6. Padányi, Viktor A nagy tragédia I. (The great tragedy vol I.), Minerva Books, 1977, pg 213.

7. Sulyok, Dezső Magyar tragédia I. (Hungarian Tragedy vol. I.) Newark, 1954, pg 164.

8. Padányi, Viktor A nagy tragédia I. (The great tragedy vol I.), Minerva Books, 1977, pg 286.

9. Welles, Sumner The time of decision. New York, pg 79

10. Churchill, Winston The Gathering Storm, London, pg 289

11. Padányi, Viktor A nagy tragédia I. (The great tragedy vol I.), Minerva Books, 1977, pg 289.

12. Sulyok, Dezső Magyar tragédia I. (Hungarian Tragedy vol. I.) Newark, 1954, pg 170.

13. Borsody, István Benes, Budapest, Athaeneum, pg 202.

184

14. **Kossuth, Lajos** Kossuth Lajos összes munkái, I-XII (The entire works of Louis Kossuth, vols.I-XII) Budapest, 1957.

15. **Czambel S.** Ceskoslovensky Casopois Historicky (History of the Communist Czechoslovakia), 1976, pg 32

16. ibid pg 39.

17. **Vartikova, Marta** Historicky Casopis II, (History of Communism, vol. II), 1976, pg 195.

18. **Vartikova, Marta** Historicky Casopis Bratislava, (The Communist Conference of Bratislava), 1976, pg 199.

19. **Ölvendi, János** Magyarok Csehszlovákiában, Rome, 1978

20. Ibid pg 15

21. **Cas** Bratislava, October 1945.

22. **Zvara, Juraj** Madarska mensina na Slovensko pro roku 1945. Bratislava, 1969.

23. **Granatier, A.** A Felszabaditot Dél (The liberated South), Nyitra, 1946.

24. **Pravda** Bratislava, November-1st issue, 1946.

25. **Pravda** Bratislava, November - 3rd issue, 1946.

26. **Zvara, Juraj** Madarska mensina na Slovensko pro roku 1945. Bratislava, 1969. pg 168.

27. **Kettős Járom Alatt** A Csehszlovákiai Magyarok Nemzeti Bizottmányának jelentés, 1951 (The Czechoslovak Hungarian Minority Commission Report, 1951), Published in Twinsburg, Ohio, March issue 1985.

ADDENDUM

Historic Chronology
I.

Important Events
in the Political History of
the First Czechoslovak Republic
(1920 - 1939)

1920
Jan 10:

Czechoslovakia, one of the signers of the Versailles peace treaty, joins the League of Nations. Between 1920 to 1922 a ceiling is put on the size of property that can be had by medium landowners and the excess portions are distributed among planters mostly to Czechs and Moravians. In the whole country 2,857 plantations are called to existence (390 in Bohemia, 191 in Moravia and Silesia, 2,054 in Slovakia and 222 in Ruthenia).

The size of these in Slovakia and Ruthenia is 25,485 hectares (cca. 62,000 acres) and in the rest of Czechoslovakia 8,058 hectares.

Apr 18 to
Apr 25:

The first national election gives 74 mandates to the Social Democratic Party, 33 to the Czechoslovak Catholic Peoples' Party, 28 to the Republican Agrarian Party, 24 to the National Socialist Party, 19 to the National Democratic Party, 12 to the Slovakian Agrarian Party, 6 to the Tradesmen's Party, 3 to Modracsek's Socialist group, 72 to the German parties, 10 to the Hungarian Parties (Social-Democratic 4, Christian-socialists 4, small holders 2). The Tusan government secures 144 mandates against the 137 of the opposition.

May 6: The supreme council of the Allies rejects Hungary's proposition for the rectification of the frontiers (Benes and Titulescu prevail), and the peace treaty with Hungary is declared final.

May 27: The Czechoslovak National Assembly elects Masaryk as President of the Republic. (Masaryk received 284 votes out of 411.

Jun 4: The Hungarian delegates sign the Trianon peace treaty. It is the most mournful day of the history of Hungary.

Jun 15: The World Federation of Trade Unions, which is under Social democratic leadership, launches a political and economic boycott against Hungary.

Jun 20: Czechoslovakia joins the boycott. The social democrat emigres of the infamous revolution of Hungary support the proposition in the Prague parliament.

Aug 14: On the initiative of Benes, an agreement between Czechoslovakia and Yugoslavia is signed in Belgrade. It is "defensive" in character.

1921
Jan 10: Czechoslovakia, when the Allies notify the Hungarian government that the part of Western Hungary inhabited by Germans would be annexed to Austria, offers military assistance to the Austrians.

Mar 26: Benes invites Rumania to enter into alliance with Czechoslovakia and Yugoslavia. The Little Entente is formed.

Apr 17:	Benes, the Foreign Minister of Czechoslovakia, protests before the council of the Nations against a proposed investigation of an international committee into the violations of the human rights of the Hungarian minority in Czechoslovakia.
Jun 17:	In a session of the Czechoslovak Economic Council, a Slovak speaker deplores the fact that the industry on Northern Hungary has been deprived of its vitality through the expulsion of leading manufacturers. Commerce and trade in Slovakia is given colonial status.
Oct 21:	Under the name "Czechoslovenska League" a political organ is formed. It promotes the settlement of Czechs and opening of Czech schools in the Hungarian areas, for obvious reasons. As a result, thousands of unskilled Czechs settle in Slovakia.
Oct 27:	Czechoslovakia mobilizes its military forces when King Charles IV attempts to return to Hungary. Udrzal, the Minister for National Defence, proclaims martial law in Slovakia and Ruthenia.
1922 Jun 5:	A Czechoslovak-Soviet Russian treaty is signed "in the spirit of the Rapallo agreement", in the name of the Panslavic fraternity.
Aug 8:	Benes sends a note to the League of Nations in which he objects to the extension of minority rights in Czechoslovakia.

1923
Sep 16:

The local elections in the Czech and Moravian regions reflect the parliamentary balance of power. In Slovakia and Ruthenia the parties in opposition gain a number of seats. The Hlinka party receives 67 mandates, the Agrarian party 62, the three Hungarian parties 48, the communist party 23, the Social democratic party 9, the Czech national-socialist party 5, the Ruthenian agrarian party 2 mandates.

1924
During
February:

During the month of February Lord Dickinson the Chairman of the Committee of the League of Nations, and Al Ramsay visit Slovakia and Ruthenia. In their report they urge the solution of the minority problems. At the same time, Benes, in his book entitled "Problemy nove Europy a zohrauicny politika Ceskoslovenska" (The new Europe and the problems of the Czechoslovak foreign policy) expresses dissatisfaction over the frontier between Czechoslovakia and Hungary.

Feb 3:

The Czech language is declared the official language in Ruthenia. The local languages (Hungarian and Ruthenian) are allowed to be used as languages of conversation.

Jun 26:

The parliament passes a bill according to which those who lived in Northern Hungary at least four years before 1910, may apply for citizenship and cannot be expatriated until the end of the proceedings. So, the Hungarians whose ancestors lived in Northern Hungary have to apply for citizenship; and those, too, who settled there between 1910 and 1918.

Oct 22:

Jozsef Szent-Ivány, the leader of the Hungarian National Party demands guarantee of equal rights.

1928   After his tour through Slovakia, Seton Watson writes a series of articles. His conclusion is that the settlement of the minority problems in that region is desirable, for putting it off endangers the peace of the Danubian basin.

Oct 28:   Budlo A., a University professor in Prague, states that Ruthenia is part of Czechoslovakia only temporarily, for sooner or later it has to be yielded to Soviet Ukraine. It is published in the periodical "Cescoslovenska Republica".

Nov 20:   Michael Yuhasz, leader of the Russin Council of National Defense, sends the Prague   government a   memorandum   in

which he sharply criticizes the government policy in regard to the minorities.

1929   In the month of April the question of citizenship
During   is discussed.   The   discussion   produces   no
April: agreement.

Jun 10:   The Czechoslovak ambassador in Budapest lodges a protest because of the "revisionist activity" of the Hungarian government.

1939   President Masaryk, in a statement given to a
Sep 25:   reporter of "Times", mentions the possibility of peaceful territorial adjustment.

Dec 2:   According to the census conducted in Czechoslovakia, 7,446,632 Czechs lived in the state, and 7,282,904 of other nationalities (3,318,445 Germans, 2,309,972 Slovaks, 719,569 Hungarians, 568,941 Ruthenians, 204,779 Jews,

100,322 Poles, 14,170 Rumanians and 46,706 of other nationalities). Since the published data does not correspond to the actual figures, minority groups bombard the League of Nations with petitions, urging investigations. (That the Hungarian population in Pozsony, Kassa and Ungvár was under 20% was a blatant distortion.)

1931
Feb 24:

Diplomatic protest in made in Prague and Belgrade, deploring the intensive anti-Hungarian press campaign.

During
June:

Lord Robert Cecil is on a fact finding mission in Prague. After his return to London he declares that Czechoslovakia's dealing with the minorities is unfair.

1932
Mar 5:

The French Prime Minister, Tardieu, publicizes his plan. It urges the five Danubian states to regulate their export trades, paving the road toward a uniform customs policy in the Danubian basin.

Mar 22:

Benes makes the League of Nations acquainted with the plan of Tardieu. He says Czechoslovakia will not take part in any solution that might threaten the "political equilibrium" of Europe.

End of
March:

Renn Ludwig and Gerald Hamilton, returning from a tour in Ruthenia assert that there is famine in Ruthenia.

The Czechoslovak government is not at all concerned about the well-being of its citizens in that area.

1933
Feb 16:
At the initiative of Benes, the Foreign Ministers of the Little Entente decide on tightening the alliance. The proposal calls for a "diplomatic federation" of the three states, i.e. Czechoslovakia, Rumania and Yugoslavia. Another anti-Hungarian move.

Jul 4:
The U.S.S.R. and the Little Entente conclude a non-aggression pact, a sequel to the Eastern European treaty drawn up at London the previous day.

Aug 15:
During the "Pribina festivities" Andrej Hlinka reads a declaration before a crowd of hundred thousand people (in the presence of the representatives of the Czechoslovak government) in which he demands that the Pittsburg treaty be put into effect. As it has been mentioned before, Masaryk had made an agreement with the American Slovaks, promising Slovakia autonomy. Later he ate his words.

Dec 7:
Benes, on a tour in Southern Slovakia, rejects the Slovak demand of autonomy; he also censures the statements of Count István Bethlen, Prime Minister of Hungary, made on his tour in England.

1934
Jul 2:
Benes addresses the Prague parliament and speaks of the three defensive roles of the Little Entente. He refers to the fear of revision, the restoration of the Habsburg dynasty and "Anschluss".

1935
May 16:
An assistance pact with the Soviets is signed in Prague.

Dec 18:	Benes is elected President of Czechoslovakia. Géza Szülls, the leader of the Hungarian party suggests in a meeting that Benes should be kept at home in order to abate his influence over foreign politicians. The opposition parties in Slovakia and Ruthenia vote for Benes persuaded by promises made by the Foreign Minister.
1936 Mar 26:	A Bill on the defense of the republic becomes law in the Czechoslovak National Assembly. On a 25 km. wide belt along the frontiers the building of concrete air raid shelters begin. A citizen considered "untrustworthy" cannot have private property and must not be employed in institutions or factories of national import. This law affects the Hungarians in Southern Slovakia more than any others.
1937 Sep 14:	Masaryk, the founder president of the Czechoslovak republic dies in the Lana mansion.
1938 Mar 24:	Hlinka's party announces the formation of the autonomist front.
Mar 28:	Prime Minister Hodsa's radio message is broadcasted. He announces that the Czechoslovak government is preparing a "Minority statue".
Apr 4:	Andrej Hlinka proclaims his will to fight to the end for self government.
Apr 15:	The "minority statute" allows the use of a non-Czech language in administrative affairs, but local autonomy is out of the question

May 7:   Britain and France intervene in Prague. B.C. Newton and De la Croix,Plenipotentiary Ministers, confer with Foreign Minister Krofta in regard to the peaceful solution of the minority problems.

May 17:   The Hungarian minority in Pozsony requests equal rights and the right of self-government.

May 21:   Czechoslovakia mobilizes two divisions. The skilled reservists are called to arms. The mobilization on such a large scale (300,000 men are affected) is considered rash in Paris and London. The use of the Hungarian language guaranteed by the "Minority Statute" is not put into practice the way it should be, due to the falsified statistical data.

Jun 5:   P. Hletko, a Slovak repatriated from the United States, shows the original copy of the Pittsburg agreement between the Czechs and the Slovaks, 20 years after it was signed.

Aug 16:   Andrej Hlinka, leader of the Slovak People's Party and of the autonomist movement, dies in his Rózsahegy rectory.

Sep 10:   Lord Runciman having returned from Prague, says in his report that his mission as intermediator and investigator encountered insuperable obstacles.

Sep 16:   The Hungarian government protests against the mobilization at the Czechoslovak-Hungarian frontier.

Sep 17:   The United Hungarian Party demands complete self-government.

Sep 19: Chamberlain, Daladier and Bonuet accept the demands of Hitler and approve the frontier adjustment of Czechoslovakia.

Sep 21: The Czechoslovak government, after several protest by England and France, reluctantly agrees to give up the Sudeten German areas of its territory. Litvinov, a Soviet Commissar notifies the League of Nations the Soviet Union is ready to fulfil its obligations to Czechoslovakia.

Sep 22: Syrovy orders general mobilization. State of war is declared.

Sep 24: The German ultimatum is delivered in Prague.

Sep 29: Hitler, Mussolini, Chamberlain and Daladier are conferring in Munich, Germany. According to their agreement, the Sudeten German part of Czechoslovakia is to be handed over to Germany in the first ten days of October; the question of the Hungarian minority must be settled within three months.

Oct 1: The Hungarian government expresses its wish to discuss the question of frontier adjustment with representatives of the Czechoslovak government.

Oct 5: Benes resigns as President of Czechoslovakia. Sudetenland is occupied. Chamberlain makes a statement to the effect that the frontiers of Czechoslovakia will be guaranteed only after the Hungarian question is settled.

Oct 6:   At Zsolna, the Slovak People's Party proclaims the autonomy of Slovakia, on the basis of the Pittsburg agreement. The leaders of the Hlinka Party form an autonomous Slovak government, with Jozef Tiso as Prime Minister. In Pozsony, a Hungarian National Council is born which demands the adjustment of the frontiers through plebiscite.

Oct 9:   Pál Teleki, Minister of Education, and Kálmán Kanya Foreign Minister, attend a conference with Tiso and the Czechoslovak Foreign Ministry. The negotiations are based on a clause drawn up at Munich. However, the outcome is poor. The Czechoslovaks are unwilling to co-operate. Evacuation of the town of Ipolyság and of the railway station of Sátoraljaujhely is the only result.

Oct 11:   Hungarian troops march into Ipolyság and a part of Sátoraljaujhely beyond the brook named Ronyva.

Oct 13:   The negations between Czechoslovakia and Hungary are suspended.

Oct 18:   The negotiations are resumed. The Polish government sends notes to the Italian, German, Czechoslovak and Rumanian governments, demanding a common frontier with Hungary. Tiso confers with Ribbentrop, German Foreign Minister at Munich.

Oct 26:   Czechoslovakia proposes arbitration by German and Italy.

Oct 30:   Germany and Italy accept the proposal.

Nov 2:   Ciano, Italian Foreign Minister and Ribbentrop draw up the new boundary between Czechoslovakia and Hungary. A territory of 11,912 square kilometres and 1,060,000 inhabitants are returned to Hungary.

Nov 6-10:   The Hungarian troops occupy the re-annexed areas.

Nov 20:   The autonomous Slovak government holds general elections with a single list of candidates, thereby initiating a one-party system (the People's Party)

Dec 31:   The Slovak government takes a census in the territory of Slovakia. It is conducted with a bias against Hungarians. From now on the Hungarian minority is persecuted by fascist Slovaks.

1939
Jan 6:   Czech military units attack Munkács. They are driven back.

Jan 7:   The Prague central government demands oath of allegiance from the autonomous Slovak government. The Slovak Council of Ministers rejects the demand.

Jan 10:   There are demonstrations against Hungary in Czechoslovakia. In Pozsony, the demonstrators ravage the editorial office of the newspaper "Esti Ujság".

Mar 10:   Upon the orders of the Prague government the Besztercebánya Army Corps occupies the valley of the rivers Vág the cities of Pozsony and Zsolna, and martial law is declared in Slovakia. The Slovak autonomists provide the police squads of the Hlinka party with arms.

Mar 13:   Tiso, the Slovak President, pays a visit to Hitler. The Fuhrer and his foreign Minister, Ribbentrop, agree to the secession of Slovakia from the Czechoslovak Republic.

Mar 17:   Tiso asks Hitler to defend Slovakia, Hitler accepts the invitation and signs a pact. German troops enter Slovakia and occupy the region west of the river Vág.

Mar 20:   A Slovak decree   allows one Hungarian and one Ruthenian representative in the parliament. Thus Slovakia is turn into a one-party fascist state, thanks to Hitler. The Prague Czechoslovak parliament is dissolved. Czech-Moravia becomes a German protectorate.

Mar 23:   Germany guarantees the independence of Slovakia for 25 years. (It last 5 years...)

Historic Chronology
II.

The Main Events
of the Second World War
(1939-1945)

1939

Sep 1:   Germany invades Poland

Sep 3:   England and France declares war on Germany.

Sep 5:   The Germans occupy the Danzig corridor.

Sep 17:   Soviet troops occupy Poland.

Sep 18:   The Polish government is moved from Lublin to Lemberg, then later to Kuty. (A village near the frontier of Rumania), and finally to Rumania where the members of the government are interned.

Sep 27:   Warsaw falls.

Sep 29:   Germany and the Soviet Union agree to have a common frontier. The Soviet Union makes an agreement with Estonia where it sets up military bases.

Nov 3:   The attempt of Hitler's life fails.

Nov 30:   The war between Finland and the Soviet Union breaks out.

1940

Mar 12:   the Finns accept the Soviet terms of peace: The Finns give up the Karelian Isthmus with the city of Viipuri, allow setting up military bases on the peninsula Hanko and yield some areas north of the lake Ladoga.

Mar 28:   The English and French Governments agree to consult each other before peace negotiations.

Apr 9:   Germany occupies Denmark and Norway.

May 10:   Chamberlain resigns, Churchill takes over. Germany occupies Netherlands and Belgium.

May 14:   The Germans bomb Rotterdam. 50,000 victims, 30,000 of them dead. Netherlands surrenders.

May 28:   Belgium surrenders.

Jun 3:   The Germans march into Dunkerque. The Belgian army surrenders.

Jun 10   Italy declares war on England and France.

Jun 14:   The Germans march into Paris.

June 15:   The Germans break through the Maginot line. The Soviet troops march into Kaunas and Vilno.

Jun 16:   Marshall Petain assumes command in France. Two days later General de Gaulle urges the French to continue the fight. France asks for a truce. The Soviet troops march into Riga and Tallinn.

Jun 18:   Churchill announces that Great Britain will fight on, if necessary for years, alone if the others quit.

Jun 22:   *The German-French armistice is signed*

Jun 24:   The Italian-French armistice is signed in Rome.

Jul 11:   Field Marshal Petain assumes the sphere of powers that the President of the Republic, Lebrun, had before.

Jul 21:   The Baltic states are annexed to the Soviet Union.

Aug 16:   Negotiations between the Hungarians and Rumanians in Turin-Severin.

Aug 30:   the Northern part of Transylvania returns to Hungary through the decision of a Wienna arbitration Court.

Sep 4:   The Constitution is suspended in Rumania. Antonescu forms a new government.

Sep 6:   The Rumanian King, Carol II, abdicates. Michael I becomes his successor.

Sep 7:   Bulgaria and Rumania sign an agreement on South Dobrudja. The Bulgarian troops occupy the area.

Sep 27:   Japan becomes an ally of Germany and Italy.

Oct 8:   Germany sends troops to Rumania.

Oct 28:   Italy attacks Greece.

Nov 5:   Roosevelt is elected President of the United States the third time.

Dec 4:   A German-Rumanian pact is signed with a promise of economical cooperation.

Dec 12:   the Hungarian Yugoslav pact of friendship is signed in Belgrade.

1941

Feb 15   Between the February 15 and November 27 the British forces recover Abyssinia from the Italians.

Apr 3:   Prime Minister Pál Teleki, seeing the extreme peril into which Hungary has been drawn, commits suicide. László Bárdossy succeeds him as Prime Minister.

Apr 6:   The Germans occupy Yugoslavia.

Apr 11:   The Hungarian army marches into Bácska.

Apr 27:   The German army marches into Athen.

Jun 22:   Germany attacks the Soviet Union. Rumania declares war on the Soviets.

Jun 23:   Hungary breaks diplomatic relations with the Soviet Union.

Jun 27:   Lászlo Bárdossy announces in Parliament that Hungary is at war with the Soviet Union. The Hungarian "Kárpát" group begins the occupation of Southern Galicia vacated by the retreating Soviet forces.

Aug 18:   Roosevelt and Churchill sign the Atlantic Charter in the vicinity of Newfoundland. The Germans are approaching Leningrad.

Aug 25:   The British and Soviet troops march into Iran.

Sep 19:   The Germans occupy Kiev. The Bitish troops march into Teheran, ahead of the Russians.

Oct 16:   The Germans occupy Odessa.

Oct 24:   Kharkov falls.

Nov 7:   The United States armours its commercial ships.

Nov 13:   The American troops occupy Island.

Dec 7:   The Japanese attack the American navy at Pearl. Harbour.   Hungary finds itself at war with Britain.

Dec 8:   The United States, England and China declare war on Japan.

Dec 11:   Germany and Italy declare war on the United States.

Dec 22:   The Japanese occupy the Philippine Islands.

Dec 25:   The Japanese occupy Hong Kong

1942

Jan 15:   Japanese-American conference in Rio de Janeiro. November.

Jan 21:   The German general Rommel launches a counter attack in North Africa.

Feb 15:   England gives up Singapore.

Mar 9:   The government of Bardossy resigns.   Miklos Kallay succeeds him as Prime Minister of Hungary.

During
April: The Second Hungarian Army advances at Kursk.

May 4:   The British troops occupy the Island of Madagascar.

May 26:   England and the Soviet Union enter into a pact to assure the cooperation of the two states for 20 years.

May 30:   Air raids by the British Air Force on Cologne and Essen, with 1,000 bombers.

Jun 1-3   The British air raids continue.

Jun 4:   The United States and Hungary are on war footing.

Jun 13:   The Germans attack Vorenezh, Rostov and Stalingrad, and also the oil fields in the Caucasus.

Oct 23:   In North Africa, the British counterattack under General Alexander and General Montgomery is successful. The battle at El-Alamein is the turning point.

Nov 8:   American troops land in North West Africa and occupy Casablanca, Oman and Algiers.

1943

Jan 12:   After a break-through at the Don river, the catastrophic retreat of the Hungarian troops begin. They would never again engage in operations against regular Soviet forces.

Jan 14:   Roosevelt and Churchill meet in Casablanca. Girand and de Gaulle participate in their discussions.

Jan 27:   The first American air raid on Germany.

Feb 2:   The Soviet troops annihilate the 6th German army at Stalingrad.

Mar 1:   Between the Mar 1st until December 31st - the British Air Force carries out 96 major air raids on 29 German industrial cities.

May 13:   The Axis Powers lay down their arms in North Africa.

Jun 10:   The Allies attack Sicily.

Jul 24:   Hamburg is bombed.

Jul 25:   Mussolini resigns, Marshal Badoglio takes over. Victor Emanuel becomes the army commander.

Aug 10:   Roosevelt and Churchill confer in Quebec.

Sep 3:   The Allies land at Reggio di Calabria and in Siracusa an armistice is signed.

Sep 9:   The Allies land at Napoli(Naples).

Sep 11:   The Italian navy surrenders.

Oct 13:   Italy declares war on Germany.

Oct 30:   The Four Big Powers (England, United States, Soviet Union and China) declare in a communique given after a conference in Moscow, that they wish to continue their cooperation after the war. They would set up an international organization in which all member states have an equal voice. All peaceful states could join this organization. Its purpose would be to maintain peace among nations.

Nov 9:   The auxiliary and preparatory organization of the United Nations is set up with the participation of 44 states.

Nov 22:   Roosevelt, Churchill and Chang-Kai-Sek confer in Cairo.

Nov 28:   The conference at Teheran takes place.
Roosevelt, Churchill and Stalin take part.

1944

Feb 20   Between the 20th and the 26th - the American Air
Force paralyzes 15 German air plane factories by
dropping 11,000 tons of bombs.

Mar 13:   The Soviet troops reach Rumania and advance
toward the Carpathians.

Mar 19   The Kallay government resigns. The successor of
Kallay is Dome Sztojay. Hungary is occupied by
he Germans.

Apr 3:   During this month the first Hungarian army is
assigned to defend the Carpathians, in response to
the demand of Germany.The first American air
raid on Budapest, especially on Csepel.

May 1:   The Prime Ministers of the British
Commonwealth confer in London.

May 12:   The 5th and 8th British Armies attack in Italy.

Jun 4:   Rome is liberated.

Jun 6:   The Allied forces land in France

Jun 16:   Between the 16th of June, 1944 and the 27th of
March, 1945, the Germans send 9,000 V-1's to
London and Southern England.

Jul 20:   German generals conspire against Hitler. Hitler
escapes. The national-socialist party controls the
army.

Jul 27:   Between the July 27 and August 31 - the Allies steadily advance. Caen, Granville and Auraches fall.

Aug 2:   Turkey breaks its diplomatic and economic ties with Germany.

Aug 6:   The Americans reach the river Loire.

Aug 15:   The Americans land between Nizza and Marseilles. Toulon, Avignon and Valence are liberated. The Americans march into Grenoble.

Aug 23:   The Allies sign an armistice with Rumania at their request.

Aug 25:   - Rumania declares war on Germany.
             - Paris is liberated. At the end of August the 7 German army is conquered. The German losses amount to 400,000 in North-West France.

Aug 31:   The Red Army marches into Bucharest. Sedan falls.

Sep 3:   The Red Army reaches the Danube.

Sep 11:   The Canadian and British troops march into Holland. The Hungarians cabinet decides to lay down the arms.

Sep 12:   The two American armies are united and enter Germany, north of Trier. Leltavre falls.

Sep 16:   On the 16th - the Allies land in Dalmatia. In the name of the United Nations, Marshal Malinovsky promises North Transylvania to the Rumanians if they yield Bessarabia and Northern Bukovina to the Soviet Union.

Oct 6:   The Red Army crosses the Hungarian border and advances toward the river Tisza.

Oct 11:   Russian and Rumanian troops march into Kolozsvar. In Moscow the Hungarian delegation signs the preliminary truce agreement. This meant to be the basis to going over to the Allies.

Oct 15:   Miklos Horthy, the Regent of Hungary, talks to the nation through radio and announces his decision to ask the Red Army for armistice.

Oct 16:   The Germans force the abdication of Horthy and put the Hungarian Nazi party in power.

Oct 18:   Hitler orders to set up the "Volkstrum". All German males between 16 and 60 years become liable to military service.

Oct 19:   -Between the October 19, 1944 and the 11th of March, 1945, the Americans retake the Philippine Islands.)
-On the 21st - the Red Army approaches Debrecen and reaches the river Tisza.
-Between 1944 and Mar 11, 1945, the Americans retake the Philippine Islands.

Nov 2:   The Red Army reaches the South border of Budapest.

Dec 22:   Miklós Béla Dálnoki forms a new government in Debrecen.

Dec 24:   The siege of Budapest begins.

1945

Jan 18   The Red Army marches into Pest.

Jan 21:   The Hungarian-Russian armistice is signed in Moscow.

Feb 4:   Between January 4 and 12 Roosevelt, Churchill and Stalin have a conference at Yalta. They agree on the voting method of the Security Council, Secret agreement on the division of Europe?

Feb 13:   Buda falls. The whole city is seized by the Russians.

Mar 24:   Montgomery's Army crosses the Rhine. The German losses amount to 250,000.

Apr 4:   The Red Army's military operations in Hungary come to an end. The whole country is under Soviet occupation.

Apr 12:   D. Franklin Roosevelt dies. Harry S. Truman becomes the President of the United States.

Apr 18:   The Americans march into Czechoslovakia.

Apr 25:   A conference of the United Nations is held in San Francisco. Its charter would be signed by the United States on the 8th of August, by the Soviet Union of the 23rd of August, by China on the 24 of August 1945.

Apr 28:   Mussolini is murdered by partisans. The 7th American Army crosses the Austrian border at Innsbruck.

Apr 30:   The US army marches into Munich.

May 1:   Reqent Horthy falls into the hands of the American forces.

May 2:   Berlin falls. The Austro-German military forces in Northern Italy and Tyrol surrender to general Alexander.

May 3:   Hamburg is occupied by the British forces. Also Burma in Asia.

May 4:   The German military units in Holland, Denmark and North-West Germany surrender to general Montgomery. Slovakia is occupied by the Soviet Union. The "independence" of the fascist Slovakia comes to an end.

May 5:   The left wing of the German army (400,000) surrenders to general Eisenhower. (The war lasted 5 years and 8 months. The cost was 275 billion dollars to the States.)

May 8:   General Zhukov marches into Berlin. The Red Army takes 1,060,000 prisoners of war, among them 91 generals.

May 29:   Czechoslovakia yields Sub-Carpathian to the Soviet Union.

May 30:   Bocek Bohumil, a Czechoslovak General, says that the structure and armament of the new Czechoslovak army is identical with those of the Red Army.

Jun 26:   The representatives of the five Great Powers and 46 medium and small states sign the Charter of the United Nations.(Poland joins them later.)

Jul 14   The Allied Navy bomb Japan. During the attack that last 21 days Japan loses more than 1,000 ships and 1257 air planes.

Jul 26:   Truman, Churchill and Chang-Kai-Sek send an ultimatum to Japan.

Aug 5:   An atomic bomb is dropped on Hiroshima.

Aug 8:   The Soviet Union declares war on Japan.

Aug 9:   Another atomic bomb is dropped on Nagasaki.

Aug 14:   Japan unconditionally surrenders, 3 years and 250 days after Pearl Harbor.   (The Allies disarm around 7,000,000.)

Sep 2:   The United States recognizes the provisional Hungarian government.

Sep 15:   Zoltán Tildy forms a new government in Hungary.

1946

Feb 1   The Hungarian Republic is proclaimed.   Its President is Zoltán Tildy.

Hungarian Heads of State

Kings of other dynaties:

Przemysl Vencel	1301-1304
Wittelsbach Ottó	1305-1308
Anjou Károly Róbert	1308-1342
Nagy Lajos	1342-1382
Mária	1382-1385 (1)
Kis Károly	1385-1386
Luxemburgi Zsigmond	1387-1437
Habsburg Albert	1437-1439
Jagelló Ulászló I.	1440-1444
Interregnum	1444-1453
Ruler Hunyadi János	1446-1453
Habsburg László V.	1453-1457
Hunyadi Mátyás I.	1458-1490
Jagelló Ulászló II.	1490-1516
Lajos II.	1516-1526
Zápolyai János	1526-1540

Habsburg rulers:

Ferdinand I.	1526-1564
Miska	1564-1576
Rudolf	1576-1608
Mátyás II.	1608-1619
Ferdinand II.	1619-1637
Ferdinand III.	1637-1657
Lipót I.	1657-1705
Jozsef I.	1705-1711
Károly III.	1711-1740
Mária Terézia	1740-1780
Jozsef II.	1780-1790
Lipót II.	1790-1792
Ferenc I.	1792-1835
Ferdinand V.	1835-1848
Ference Jozsef I.	1848-1916
Károly	1916-1918

Heads of State:

Count Mihály Károlyi- President of the Republic from
January 15, to March 21, 1919.

Peoples' Council- from March 21, to
August 1, 1919.

Joseph Royal Prince- "Homo Regius" from August 6,
to the end of August, 1919 .

Miklós Horthy- Regent, from March 1, 1920,
to October 16, 1944

Ferenc Szálasi- from October 16, 1944
to March 12, 1946.

Béla Zsedényi- Leader of the National Council
from December 20, 1944
to February 1, 1946.

Zoltán Tildy- President of the Republic
from February 1, 1946
to July 30, 1948.

Árpád Szakasits- President of the Republic
from August 2, 1948
to April 24, 1950.

Sándor Rónai- President of the Republic
from April 26, 1950
to August 14, 1952.

István Dobi- President of the Republic
from August 14, 1952
to March 19, 1967.

Pál Losonczi-   First Prime Minister
from March 19, 1967

Reigning Princes in Transylvania:

János Zsigmond	1540-1571	
Báthori István	1571-1576	
Báthori Kristóf	1576-1581	
Báthori Zsigmond	1581-1597	
Bocskai István	1605-1606	
Rákóczi Zsigmond	1606-1608	
Báthori Gábor	1608-1613	
Bethlen Gábor	1613-1629	
Brandenburgi Katalin	1629-1630	
Rákóczi György I.	1630-1648	
Rákóczi György II.	1648-1660	
Rhédei Ferenc	1658-1659	
Barcsay Ákos	1659-1660	
Kemény Zsigmond	1660-1662	
Apafi Mihály I.	1662-1690	
Apafi Mihály II.	1690-1695	(2)
Thököly Imre	1690-1691	(3)
Rákóczi Ferenc II.	1705-1711	(4)

Notes:

1) Co-ruler, until 1395, first with Karoly(Kis), later with Zsigmond of Luxemburg.

2) In 1681 (at age 15), he was elected. After the death of his father, a Council aided him. The emperor, however, never confirmed his position. In 1695 he was taken to Vienna.

3) The Turkish Sultan appointed him but later he was fully accepted by the Transylvania orders. His power came to an end in 1691. He attempted to regain it in 1700.

4) His father Ferenc Rakoczy I., was made Reigning Prince in 1652. He never gained the throne. He died in 1676.

Place Names

(Old Hungarian and its present Slovak Place names)

A

Alacsony-Tátra
Alsókubin (Dolná Krupá)
Aranyosmarót (Zlaté
Moravce)
Árva (Orava)
Árvaváralja (Oravskỳ
Podzámok)

B

Bártfa (Bardejov)
Besztercebánya (Banská
Bystrica)
Bős (Gabčikovo)
Breznóbánya (Brezno)

C

Csejte (Čachtice)
Cseklész (Bernolákovo)
Csorba-tó (Štrbské pleso)

D

Deáki (Diakovce)
Dévény (Devin)
Dobsina (Dobšina)
Dunaszerdahely (Dunajská
Streda)

E

Eperjes (Prešov)
Érsekújvár (Nové Zámky)

F

Felsőkubin (Výsný Kubin)
Fülek (Fil'akovo)

G

Gács (Halič)
Galanta (Galánta)
Galánta (Galanta)
Gálszécs (Sečovce)
Gölnicbánya (Gelnica)

H

Héthárs (Lipany)
Homonna (Hummenné)

I

Igló (Spišska Nova Ves)
Ilava (Illava)
Ipolyság(Šahy)

J

Jaszó (Jasov)

K

Kassa (Košice)
Késmárk (Kežmarok)
Kisszeben (Sabinov)
Komárom (Komarno)
Körmöcbánya (Kremnica)

Addendum

L
Leles (Lelesz)
Léva (Levice)
Losonc(Lučenec)
Lőcse (Levoča)

M
Magas Tátra
Magyarbél (Velký Biel)

N
Nagysáros (Vel'ký Šariš)
Nagyszombat (Trnava)
Nyitra (Nitra)

O
Ógyalla (Hurbanovo)
Ótátrafüred(StarýSmckovec)

P
Pelsőc (Plešivec)
Poprád (Poprad)
Pozsony (Bratislava)

R
Rimaszombat (Rimavská Sobota)
Rózsahegy (Ružomberok)
Rozsnyó (Rožňava)
Ruttka (Vrútky)

S
Selmecbánya (Banská Štiavnica)
Stósz (Štos)
Stószfürdő (Štos kúpele)

Sz
Szepeskáptalan, (Spišska Kapitula)
Szepesváralja (Spišske Podhradie)

T
Tátralomnic (Tatranská Lomnica)
Trencsén (Trenčin)
Turócszentmárton (Martin)

V
Vágsellye (Šal'a)

Z
Zboró (Zborov)
Zemplén (Zemplin)
Zólyom (Zvolen)

Zs
Zsolna (Žilina)

REFERENCES

Acsády,Ignác: A magyar birodalom története.
                         Budapest, 1904

Apponyi Albert: Justice for Hungary. London,
                         1928.

Benes, Eduard: Uvahy o Slovanstva. Praha, 1947.

Bernolák Antal: Lexicon slavicum, bohemico-latino-
                         germanico-ungaricum. Buda, 1825-1827.

Bernolák Antal: Lexicon Slavum. Wien, 1908 .

Bibl, V.:   Die Tragödie Österreichs.
                         Leipzig, 1937.

Bismarck, Otto: Gesammelte Werke. Berlin, 1932.
Bolváry Pál-   Magyar földrajz. Cleveland,
Kálnoky Ernő: Magyariskola, 1979.

Borsody István: Benes. Budapest, Athaenaum.

Borsody István: Magyarok Csehszlovákiában (Az
                         Ország Útja). Budapest, 1938.

Chászár Ede: A "bécsi döntés" és jelentősége (A
                         XXIII. MTk., 77-78. o.),
                         Cleveland, 1984.

Chászár Ede: A felvidéki magyarság jelenlégi
                         helyzete. (A XXIV. MTk.,
                         92-98.), Cleveland, 1985.

Addendum

Chászár Edward:

Decision in Vienna. The Czechoslovak Hungarian Border Dispute of 1938. Astor, 1978.

Dallos István - László:

Szlovenszkoi magyar irok Mártonvölgyi antologiaja. 1-4. kotet. Nyitra, 1937.

Duray Miklós:

Kutyaszoritó. New York (Püski), 1983.

Erdélyi István:

Ukrán-e a rutén? (A XVII. MTk., 57-66.o.) Cleveland, 1978.

Friedjung, H.:

Fight for German Hegemony. London, 1902.

Fischl, A.:

Der Panslavismus bis zum Weltkrieg. Stuttgart, 1930.

Grünwald Béla:

A Felvidék. Néprajzi adalék a nemzetiségi településekhez. 1896.

Cyőrffy György:

Tanulmányok a magyar állam eredétéről. Budapest, 1959.

Halkulo harangok:

A Katolikus Magyarok Vasárnapja1978-as évkönyve. Youngstown, 1979. (editor - Dunai Akos)

Haraszti Endre:

Svatopluk. A szlovák és magyar kapcsolatok kezdetei a IX. században. (A XVII. MTk, 101-112) Cleveland, 1978.

Hites Kristóf:

A Csehszlovákiai Magyarok Nemzeti Bizottsága. (A XXV. MTk. 211-214.o)Cleveland, 1986.

222

Hóman Bálint - Gyula:	Magyar történet. 6ik kiadás. I-V. Szegfű kötet. Budapest, 1939.
Hokky J. Charles:	Ruthenia Spearhead toward the West. Gainsville, 1966.
Homonnay Elemér:	Kárpátalja visszatérésének diplomáciai története. (A XVII. MTk., 47-52. o.) Cleveland, 1978.
Hunfalvy János:	A magyar birodalom néprajzi viszonyai. Budapest, 1886.
Jócsik L.:	A magyarság a cseh néprajzi térképen. Budapest, 1943.
Karácsonyi János:	Történelmi jogunk hazánk területi épségéhez. Budapest, Szeny István Társulat, 1921.
Kemény G. Gábor:	A magyer nemzetiségi kérdés története. Első rész. Budapest, 1947
Kogutowitz Manó:	Magyarország közigazgatási térképe. Mérték: 1:900.000.
Kollányi Károly:	A szlovák nép eredete, kialakulása. (A XVII. MTk., 112-13 oldal) Cleveland, 1978.
Kontz Zotán:	Kárpátalja helye az eljövendő új europai rendben. (A XVII. MTk., 52-57.o)Cleveland, 1978.
Kontz Zoltán:	Kárpátalja iskola és kultúrviszonyai. (A XV. MTk., 55-58.o)Cleveland, 1976.

Addendum

Kossuth Lajos:	Összes munkái. I-XII. kötet. Budapest, 1957 .
Kostya Sándor:	A Felvidéki Magyarok Baráti Köre. (A XXV. MTk., 213-214.o.)Cleveland, 1978
Kostya Sándor:	A Pánszlávizmus történelmi fejlődése. Toronto, 1980.
Kostya Sándor:	A pánszláv diplomácia mesterkedése a Karpát-medencebén. (A XX. MTk., 147-160.o.) Cleveland, 1984.
Kostya Sándor:	Ősi földünk, a Felvidék új történeti szemlélete. (A XXIII. MTk., 147-160.o.) Cleveland, 1984.
Kostya Sándor:	A Kárpát-medence. (A XXIV. MTk. 36-41.o.)Cleveland, 1985.
Kostya Sándor:	Panslavism. Astor, 1981.
Kostya Sándor:	Szláv világkongresszus. (A XXI. MTk., 85-91.o.) Cleveland, 1982.
Kovács Imre:	Magyarország megszállása. Toronto, 1979.
Kúz Géza:	Magyar-szlovák-cseh kapcsolat. (A IV-V. MTk., 94-112.o.) Cleveland, 1966.
Lux Andrew:	Selmecbánya. A New Interpretation of the Historic Background of Mozart's The Magic Flute. Westlake, author, 1985.

Magyar művelődés történet:	commissioned by The Hungarian Historic Society, editors: Domanovszky Sándor, Balanyi György, Mályusz Elemér,Szentpétery Imre and Varjú Elemér. Budapest, series I-V. (no date)
Magyar tájékoztató zsebkönyv:	Budapest, 1941.
Marma Gyula:	Kárpátalja önkormányzata Magyarország keretében. Az 1939 március 15-i események.(A XVII. MTk., 38-47.o)Cleveland, 1978.
Masaryk C. Thomas:	Svetové Revolucia. Praha, 1920.
Mednyánszky Alajos:	Festői utazás a Vág folyón, Magyarországon (1825). Translated by Soltész Gáspár. Bratislava, Tatran, 1981.
Nerneskürthy István:	Kik érted haltak, szent Világszabadság. A negyvennyolcas honvéd hadsereg katonaforradalmárai. Budapest, Magvető, 1977.
Padányi Viktor:	A nagy tragedia. I-II. volume. Minerva Books, 1977.
Páncélos-Pazuhanics Mihály:	A ruszinság eredete ás élete 1918-ig. (A VIII. MTk.,191-199.o)Cleveland, 1969.
Plicku, Karola:	Slovensko. Osveta, 1969.
Püspöki Nagy Péter:	Nagy-Morávia fekvése. (A XXII. MTk.,70-78. o.)Cleveland, 1983.

Addendum

Radisics Elemér:	Dunatáj. I-III. volume. Budapest, 1946.
Révai nagy lexikona:	Az ismeretek enciklopédiája. I-XXI. volume. Budapest, Révai Testvérek, 1911-1935.
Sirchich Laszló:	A Felvidék az ezeréves magyar államtestben. Magyarok Csehszlovákiában. (A XVII. MTk., 70-91) Cleveland, 1978.
Sirchich Laszló:	Belvedere-től Kassáig. A felvidéki magyarság útja az első bécsi döntéstől a "kosicky" programig. Cleveland, 1969.
Sirchich László:	A magyarság helyzete a Felvidéken. (A XII. MTk., 66-69. o.)Cleveland, 1983.
Sirchich Laszló:	Fokozódó elnemzetlenitő törekvések a Felvidéken. A felvidéki magyarság nyomorúsága és nagysága. (A XIX. MTk., 97 -111.o.)Cleveland, 1980.
Sirchich László:	Magyar művelődés a Felvidéken (A XV. MTk., 58-66.o.) Cleveland, 1976.
Somogyi Ferenc:	Küldetés. A magyarság története. Cleveland, Kárpát, 1978.
Sulyok Dezső: Szent Ivány Géza:	A magyar tragédia. Newark 1954. Magyar Felvidékönk és Kárpátalja. Pittsburgh, 1956.

Tarnay Dénes:

Autonómiát a magyarlakta
területeknek Csehszlovákiában.(A
XVII. MTk. 138-147.o)
Cleveland, 1978.

Vojatsek, Charles:

From Trianon to the First Vienna
Arbitral Award. The Hungarian
Minority in the First Czecho-
slovak Republik 1918-1938.
Montreal, 1981.

Várdy Béla:

Kárpátalja magyarsága a
csehszlovák és a szovjet uralom
alatt.(A XXIII. MTk.,78-94.o)
Cleveland, 1984.

Zvara, Juraj:

Madarska mensinu na Slovensku
pro roku 1945. Bratislava, 1969.

INDEX

Addendum

his family to leave Hungary and immigrate to Canada. After the initial difficulties of searching out a living and learning a new language, he vent on to study at the University de Montreal Faculty des lettres. There he received his M.A. for his thesis "L'Importance Litterarie et Politique du Panslavism" in 1964. Afterwards he taught Latin in Canadian highschools. During this time he established the Association of Hungarian Teachers in Canada. He succesfully formulated and taught from 1965 on a Hungarian Language and Literature course wich became accepted as a credit program at Universities. The Árpád Academy of Cleveland in 1980 awarded him a gold medal for his literary work titled, "Pan-Slavism" Presently he serves on the Board of Directors of the Toronto Hungarian Cultural Centre, where he is also the Editor of the "Krónika", a monthly literary magazine. He is a member of the Árpád Academy, Cleveland, The International P.E.N. Club and the Canadian Hungarian Authors Association, Toronto.

Dr, Kostya is the author of;

Ukrajna, Kalocsa, 1942

Our Dear Mother Tongue, Toronto, 1959,

The Hungariam ABC and Reader, Toronto, 1965,

The Modern Man, Toronto, 1979,

The Historic Emergence of Panslavism, Toronto, 1980

All in Hungarian.

Pan-Slavism, Toronto, 1980. In English.